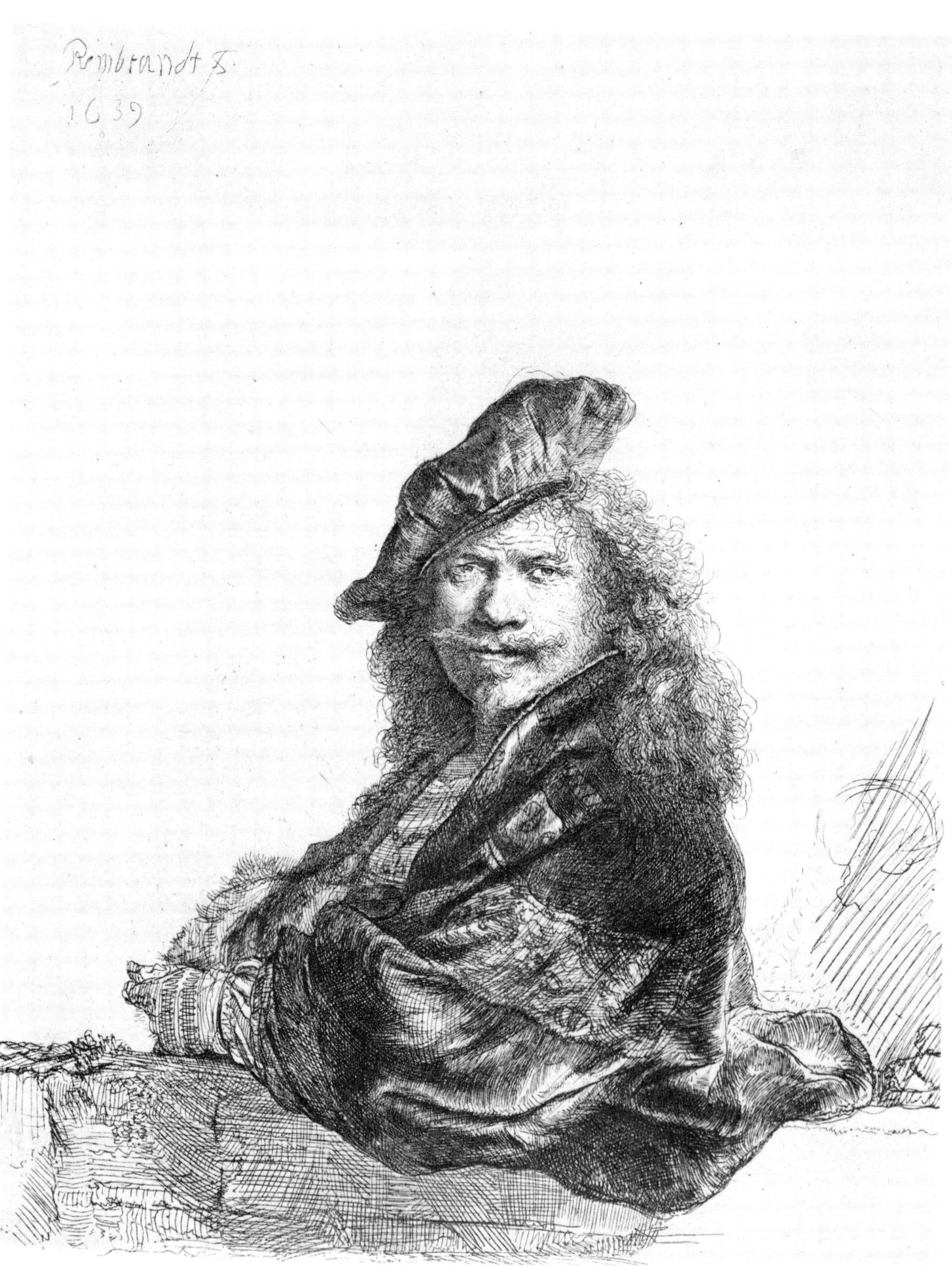

Rembrandt leaning on a stone sill. 1639.

REMBRANDT ETCHINGS

57 Illustrations

by Rembrandt van Rijn

Dover Publications, Inc.
New York

Publisher's Note

As a medium of artistic expression, etching is comparatively recent, the first dated etching having been executed by Urs Graf in 1513. Parmigianino was perhaps the earliest artist to realize the potential of etching, handling the etching needle as a pen rather than trying to use it to imitate the effects of the engraver's burin. In the North, this distinction was made slowly: Dürer's five etchings, for example, closely resemble engravings. Etching developed under such masters as Jost Amman, Lucas van Leyden and Van Dyck, but it was Rembrandt Harmenszoon van Rijn (1606–1669) who brought it to a state of perfection that has probably not been surpassed, although later artists, notably Goya and Whistler, created masterpieces in it.

Rembrandt's first dated etching was executed in 1628, the last in 1661. Using the etching needle, burin, burnisher and drypoint to obtain the effects he desired, Rembrandt developed an individual technique of great versatility. He also experimented with materials: Impressions were pulled on vellum, oatmeal paper, European papers and, from 1647, Japanese papers (the Dutch having entered into an exclusive trading arrangement with Japan in 1639).

Rembrandt sometimes labored over a plate for years, reworking it in several states. When pulling impressions of a state, he experimented with paper and the application of ink, resulting in such variety of surface tone that the effect of the work was drastically altered from one impression to another.

The etchings are reflections of Rembrandt's great humanity, made visible in his psychologically probing portraits and self-portraits, life studies, observations of daily life, the drama of his Biblical interpretations or the elegance of composition and serenity of his landscapes.

Published in Canada by General Publishing Company, Ltd.,
30 Lesmill Road, Don Mills, Toronto, Ontario.
Published in the United Kingdom by Constable and Company, Ltd.

Rembrandt Etchings: 57 Illustrations is a new work, first published by Dover Publications, Inc., in 1988.

Manufactured in the United States of America
Dover Publications, Inc.
31 East 2nd Street
Mineola, N.Y. 11501

Library of Congress Cataloging-in-Publication Data

Rembrandt Harmenszoon van Rijn, 1606–1669.
Rembrandt etchings.

(Dover art library)
1. Rembrandt Harmenszoon van Rijn, 1606–1669.
2. Etching, Dutch. 3. Etching—17th century—
Netherlands. I. Title. II. Series.
NE2054.5.R4A4 1988 769.92′4 88-3687
ISBN 0-486-25677-4

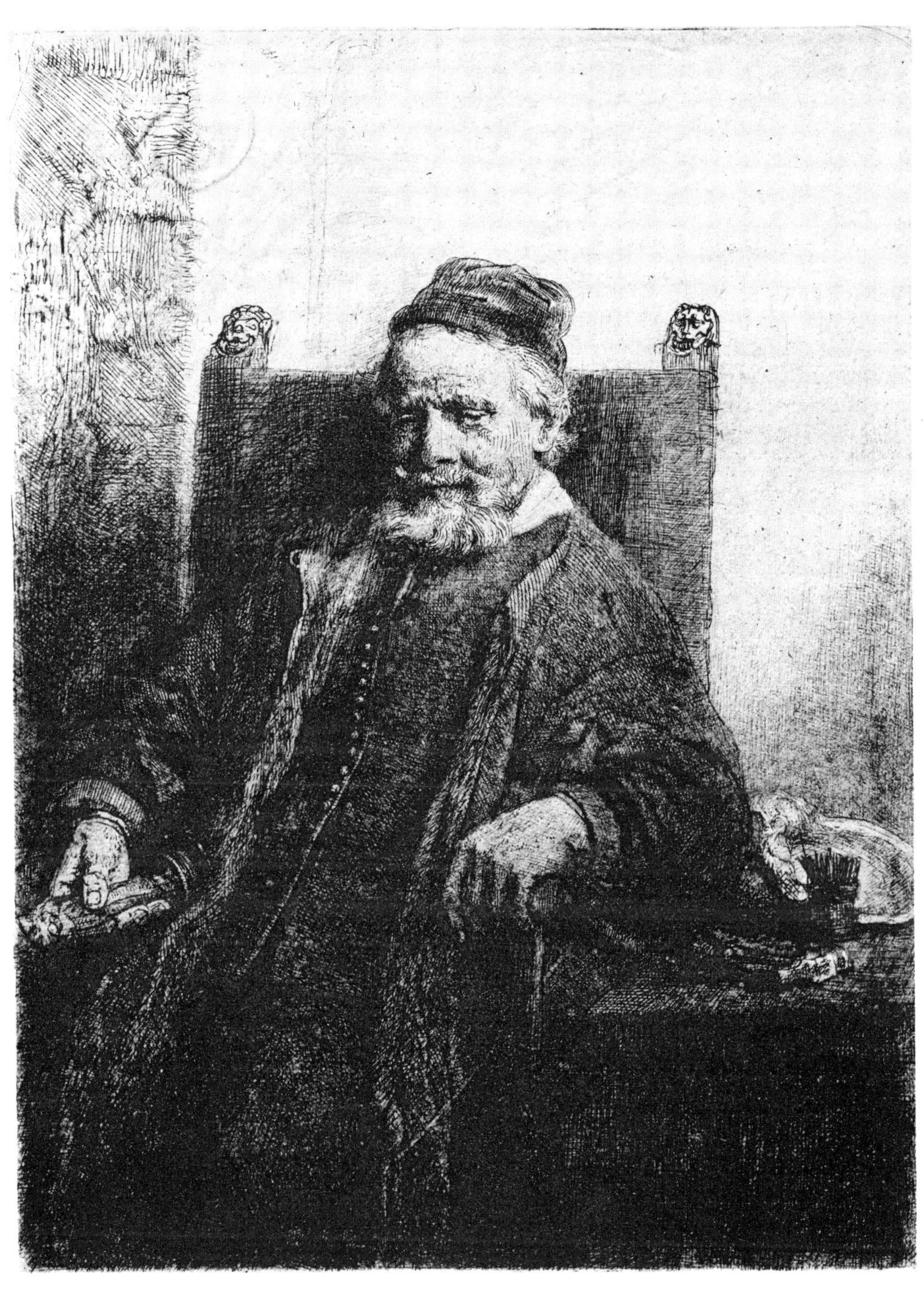

Jan Lutma the Elder, goldsmith (1584–1669). 1656.

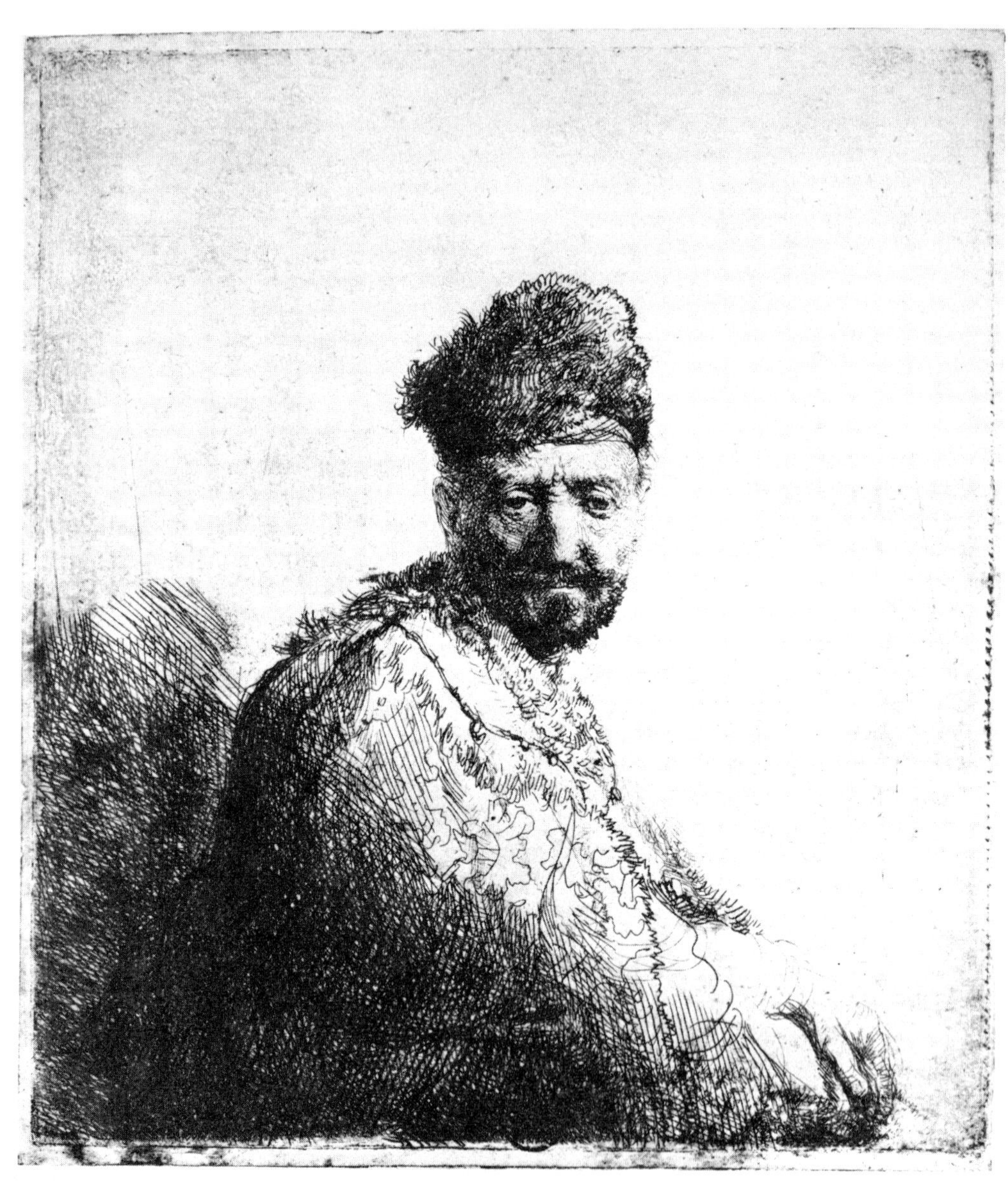

Man with a beard and fur hat. 1631.

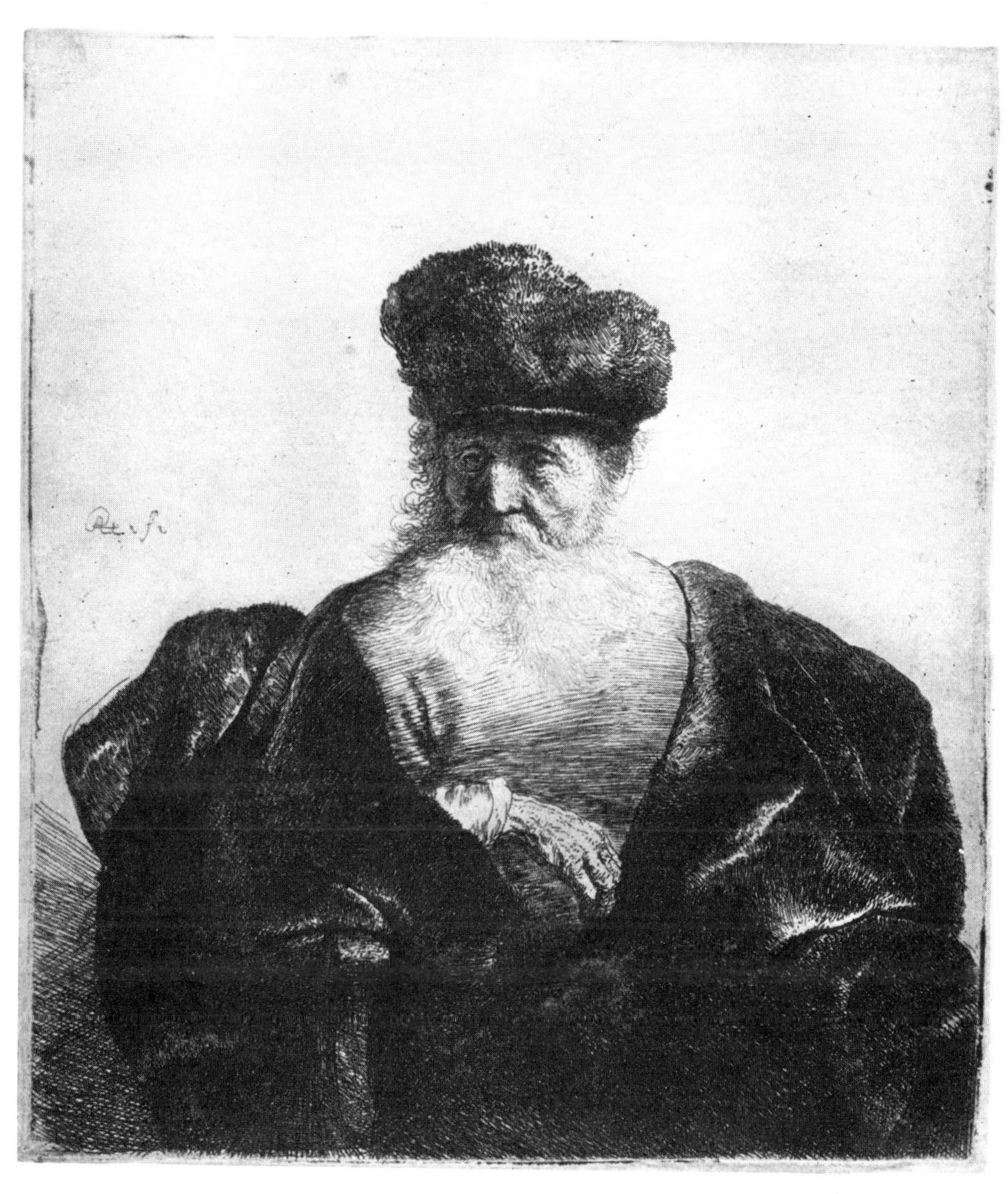

Old man with a beard, full cap and velvet cloak. 1632.

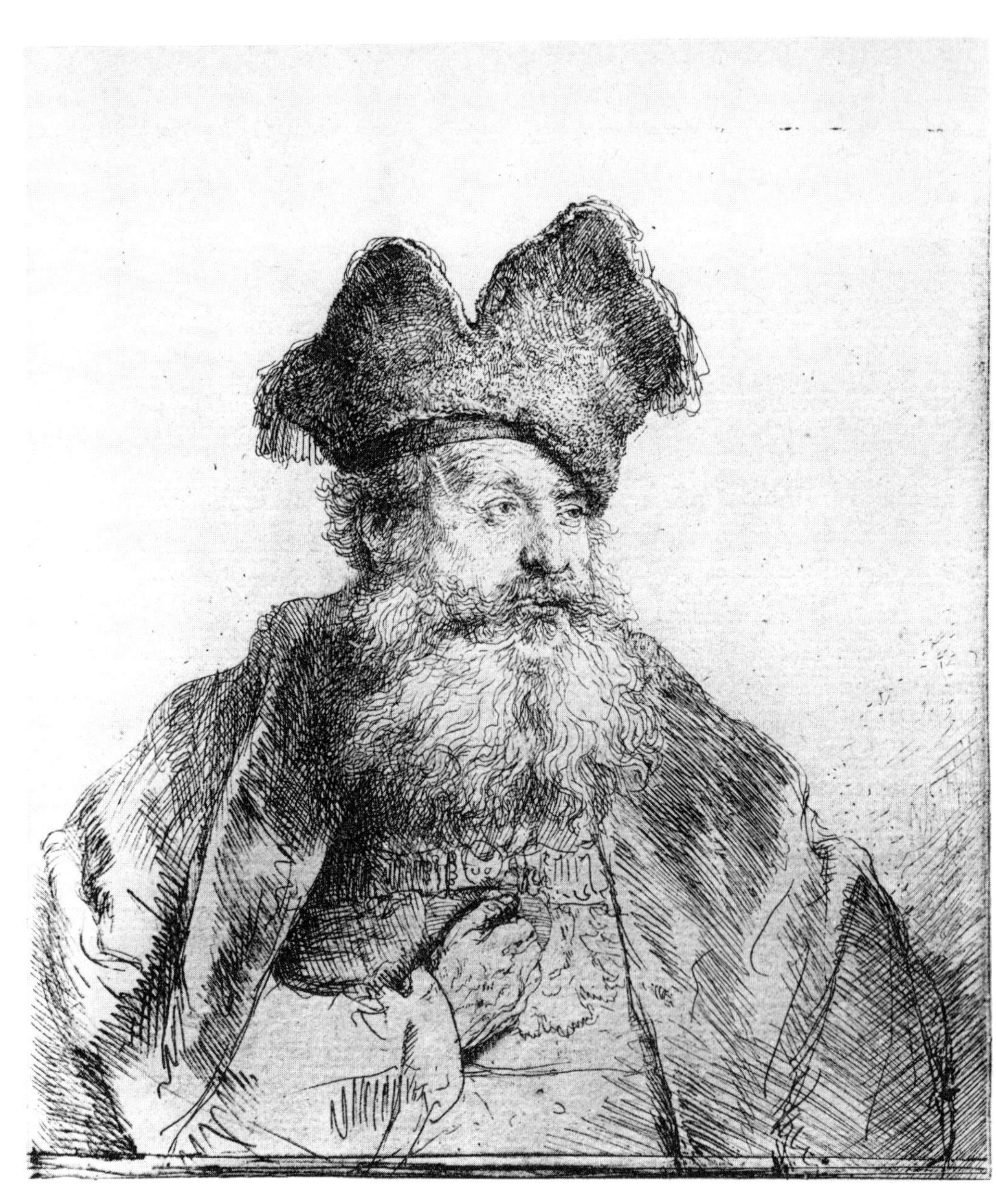

Old man with a divided fur cap. 1640.

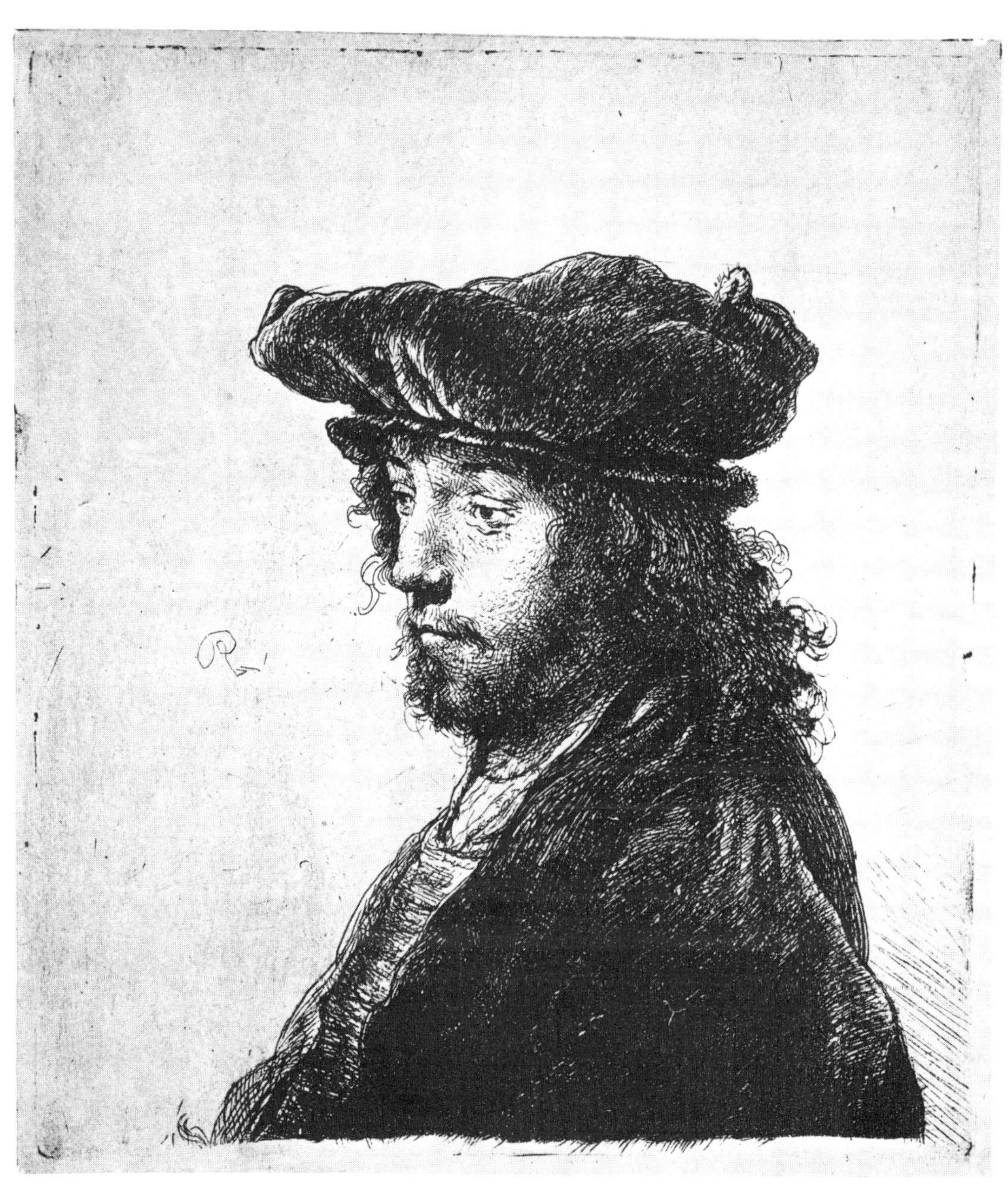

The fourth oriental head. 1635(?).

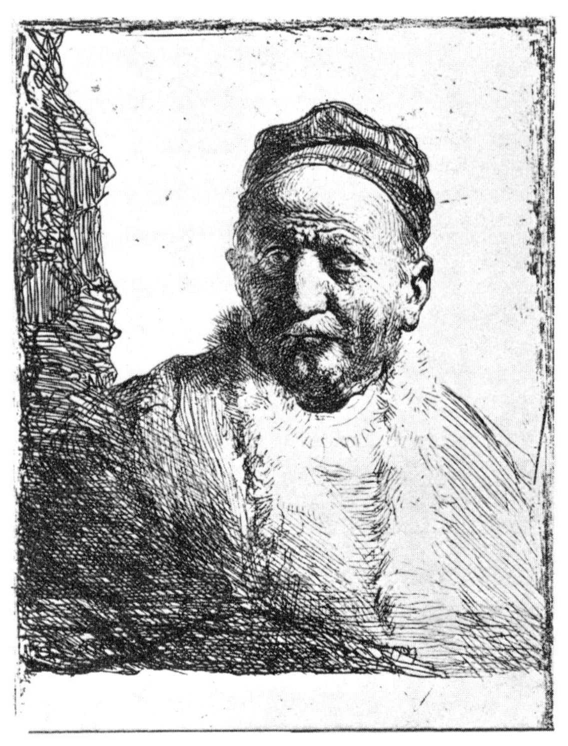

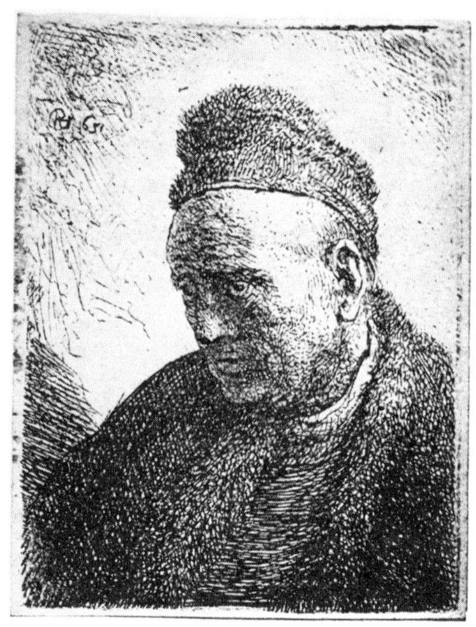

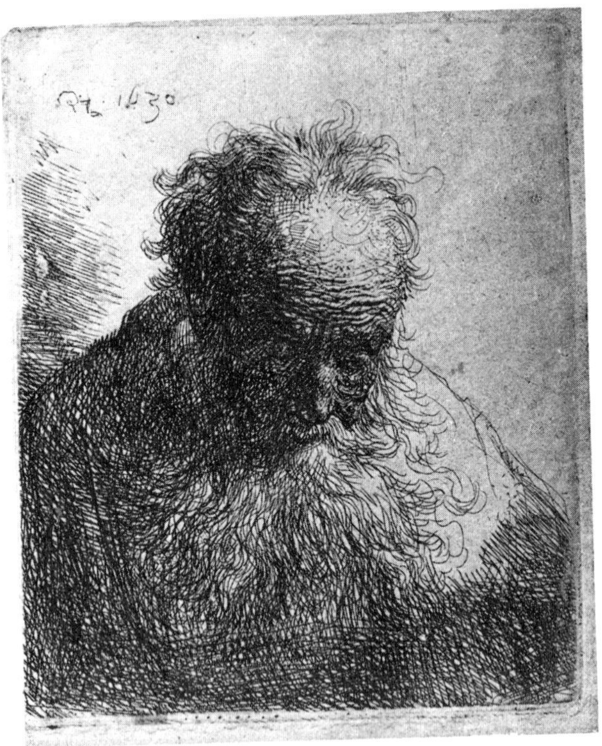

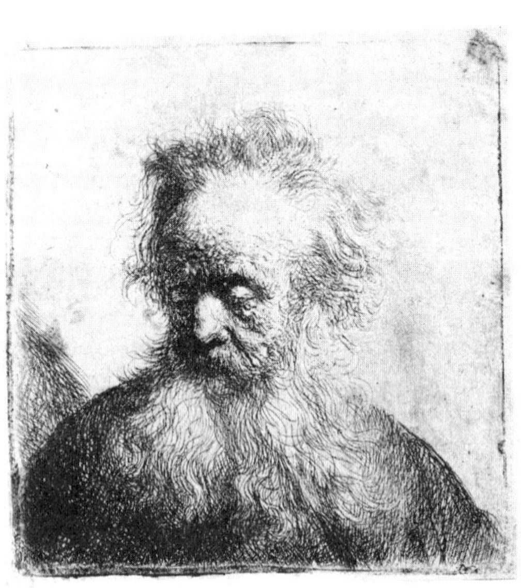

Top, left: Man wearing a close cap. 1630. *Top, right:* Beardless man in fur cap. 1631. *Bottom, left:* Old man with flowing beard. 1630(?). *Bottom, right:* Old man with flowing beard. 1631.

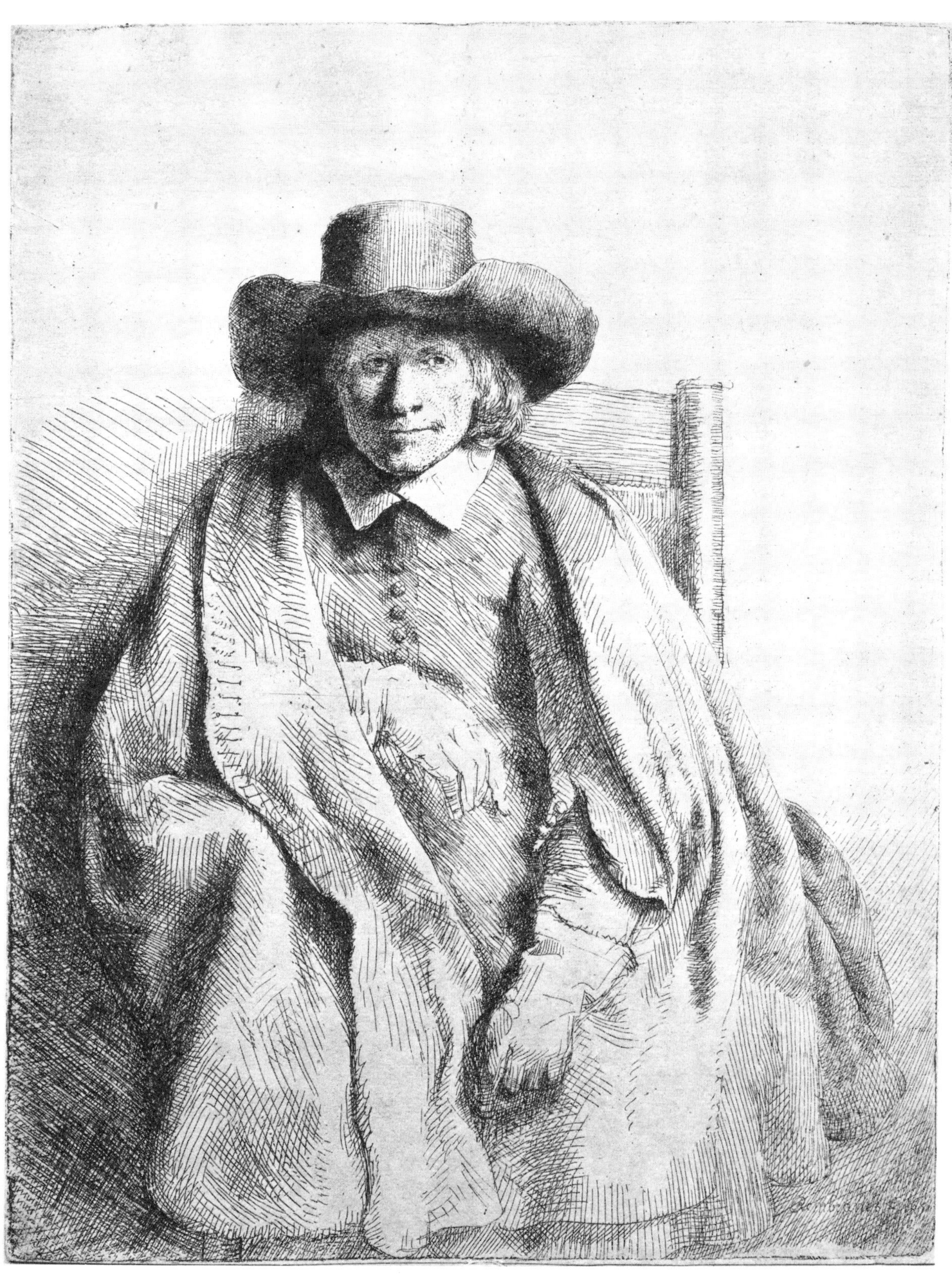

Clement de Jonghe, printseller and publisher (d. 1679). 1651.

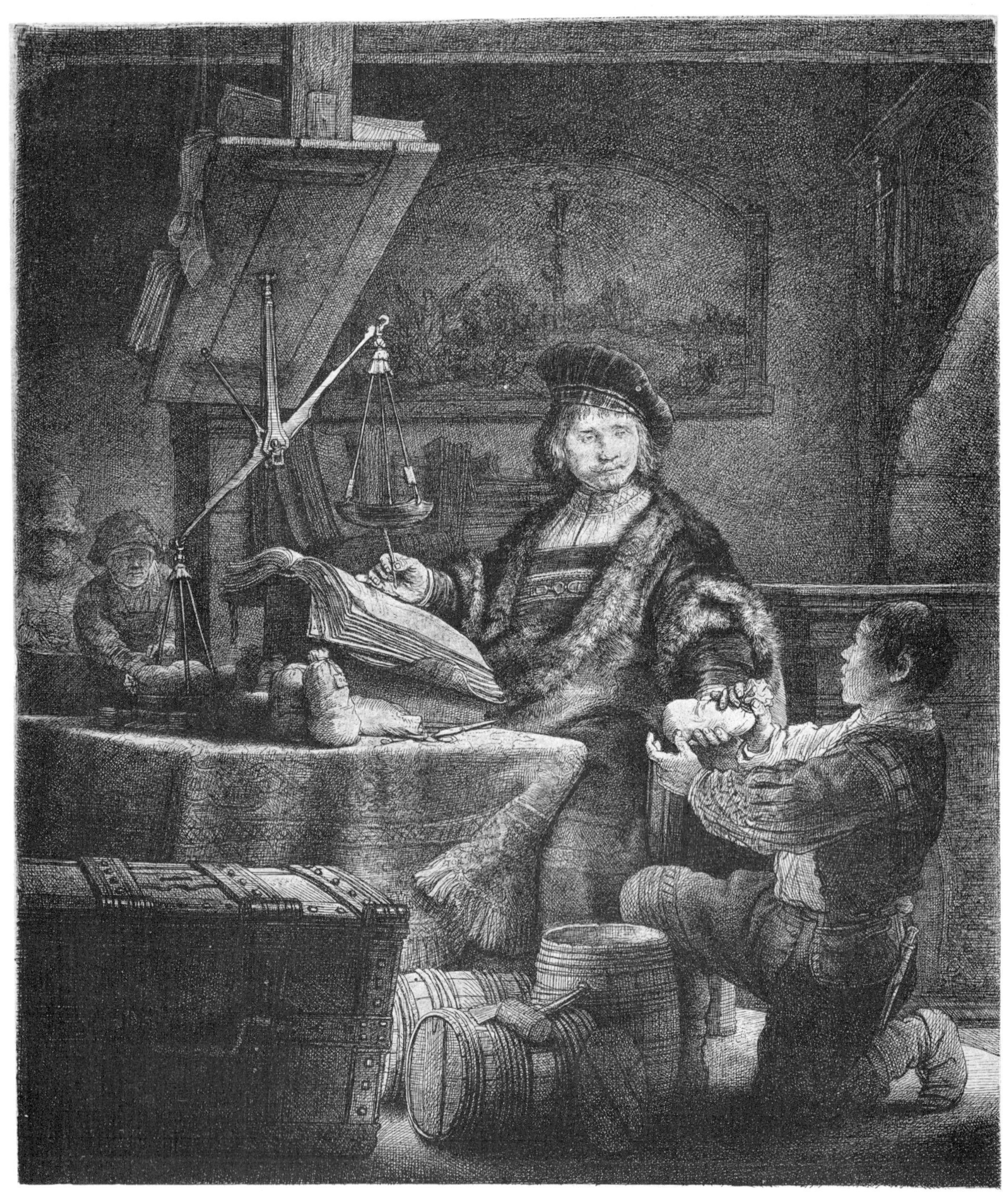

Jan Uytenbogaert, the goldweigher. 1639.

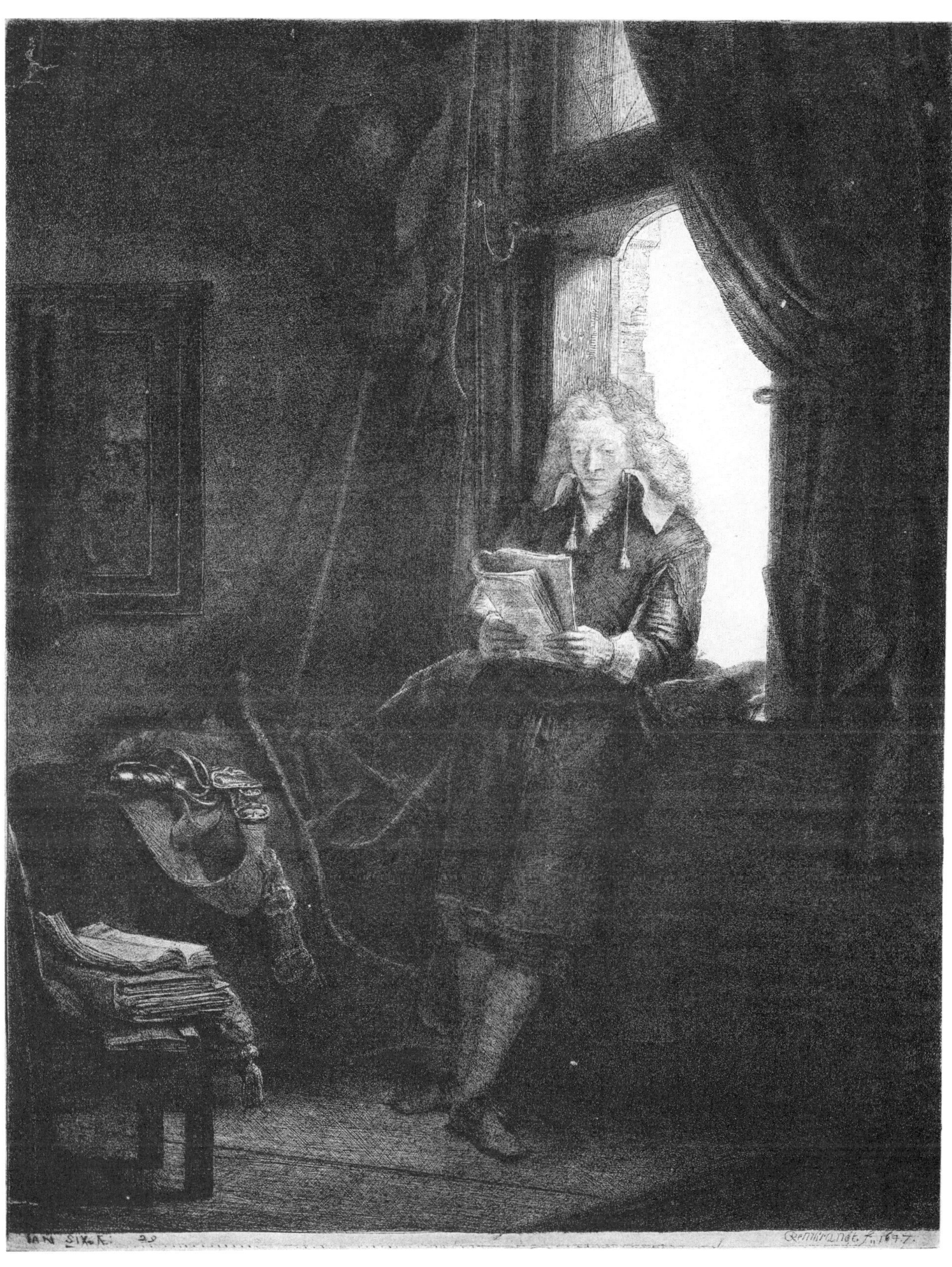

Jan Six (patron of Rembrandt; 1618–1700). 1647.

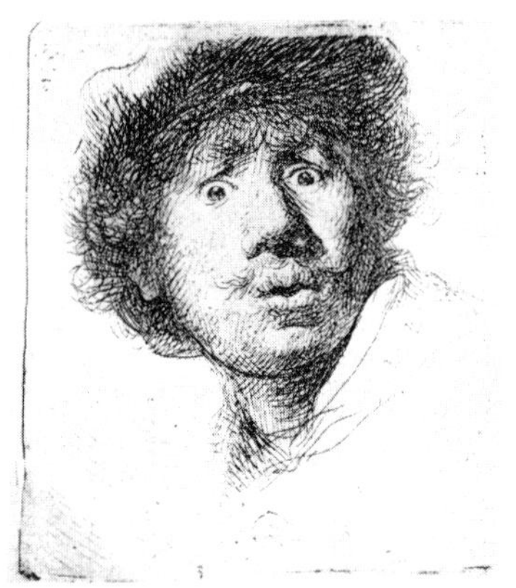

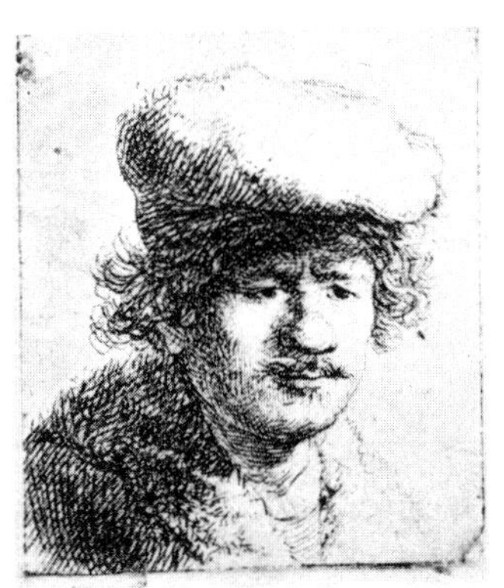

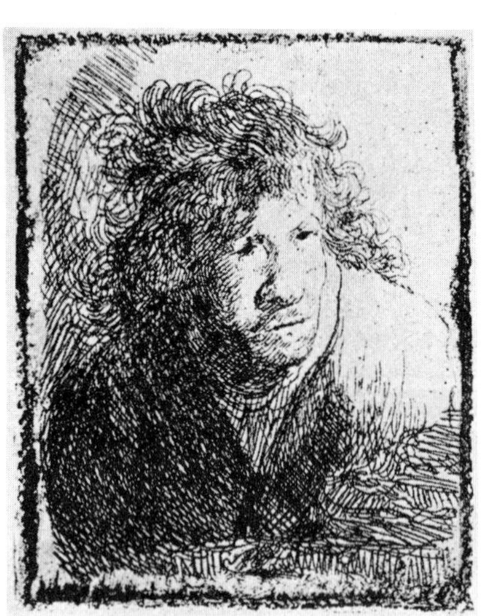

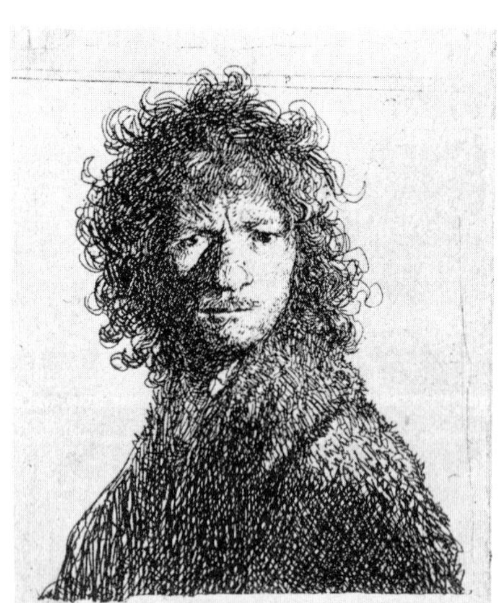

Top, left: Rembrandt in a cap, staring. 1630. *Top, right:* Rembrandt with a cap pulled forward. 1631(?). *Bottom, left:* Rembrandt, leaning forward. 1630. *Bottom, right:* Rembrandt angry. 1630.

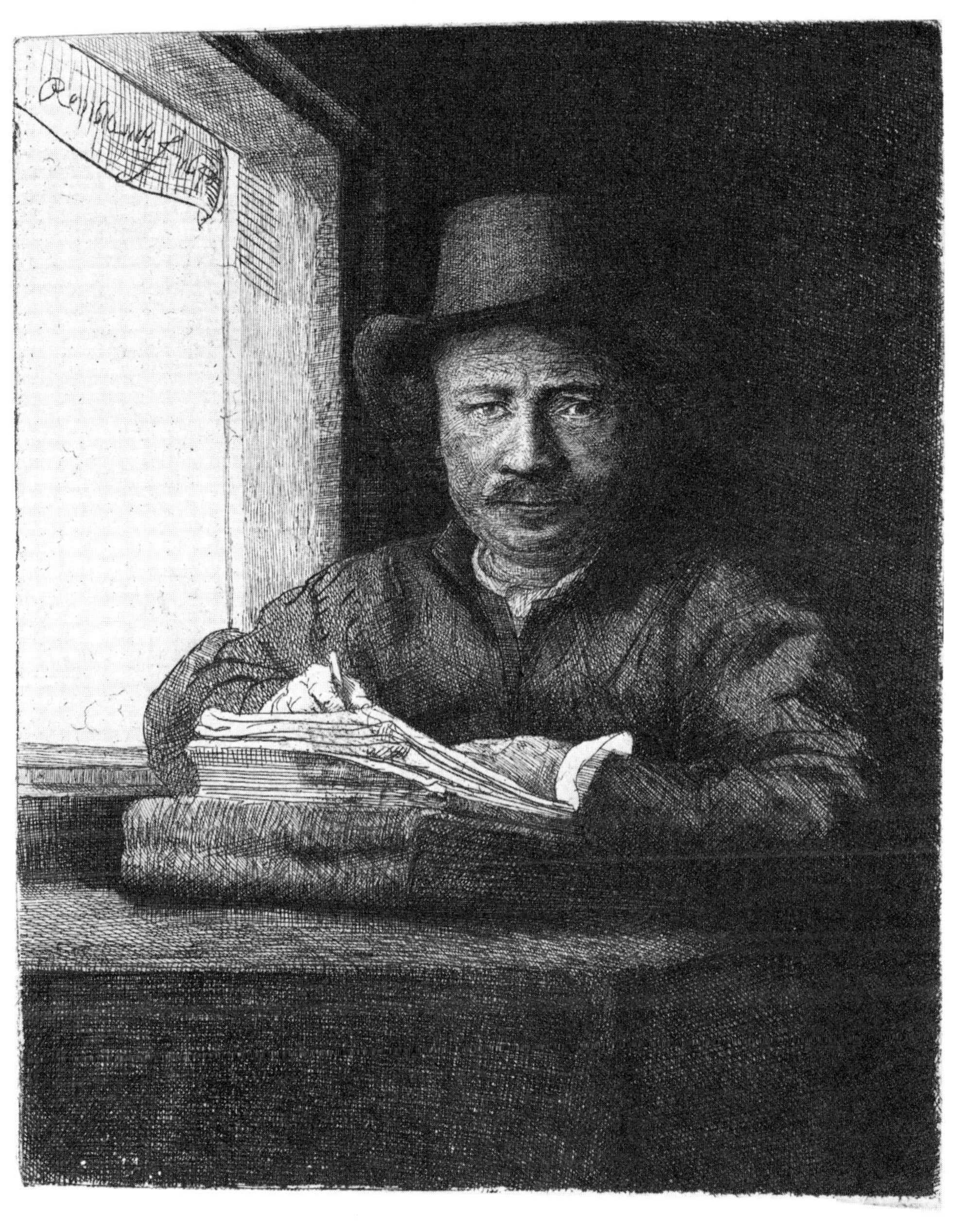

Rembrandt drawing at a window. 1648.

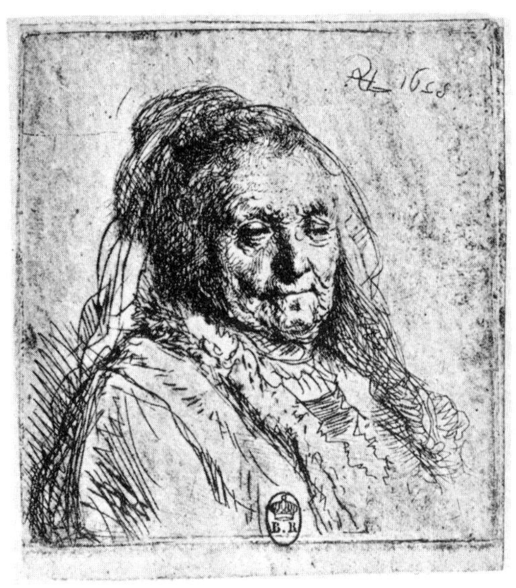

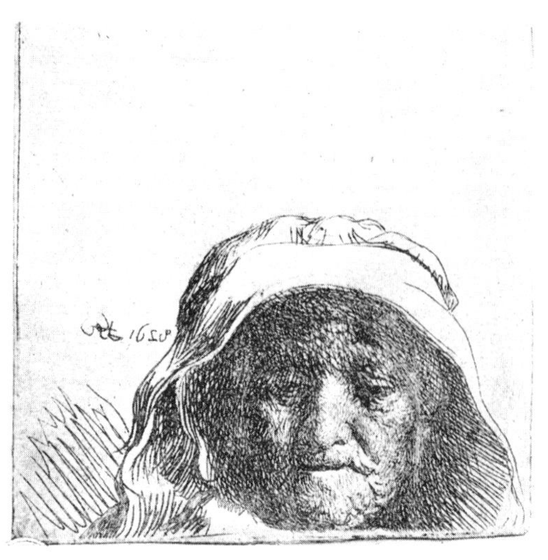

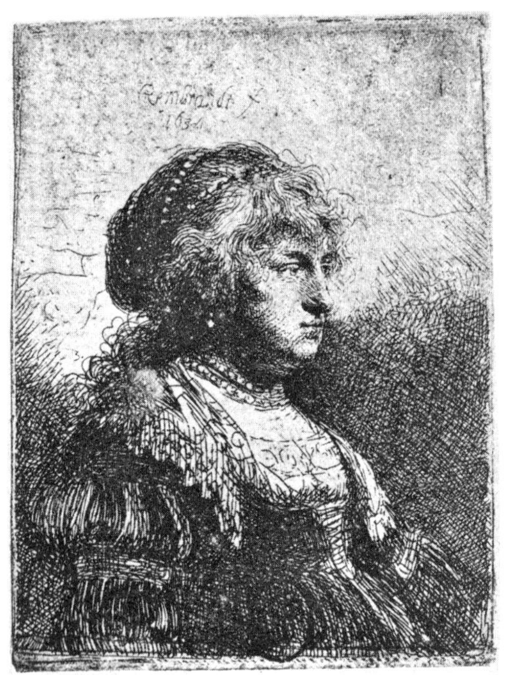

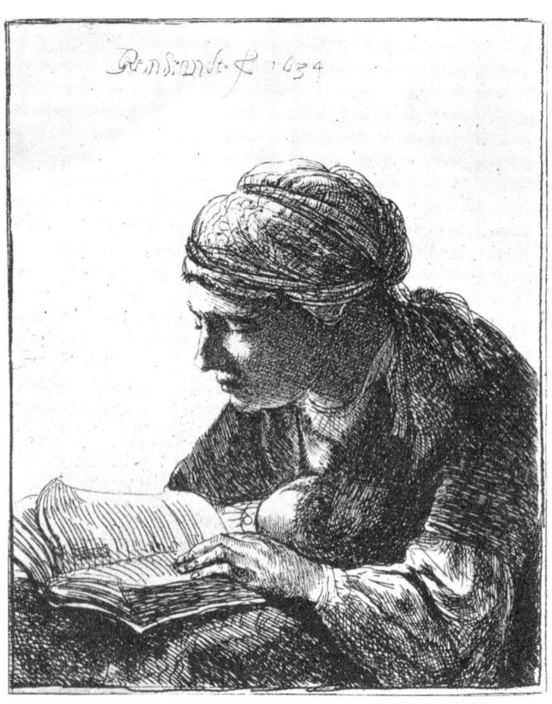

Top, left and right: Rembrandt's mother. 1628. *Bottom, left:* Saskia with pearls. 1634. *Bottom, right:* Woman reading. 1634.

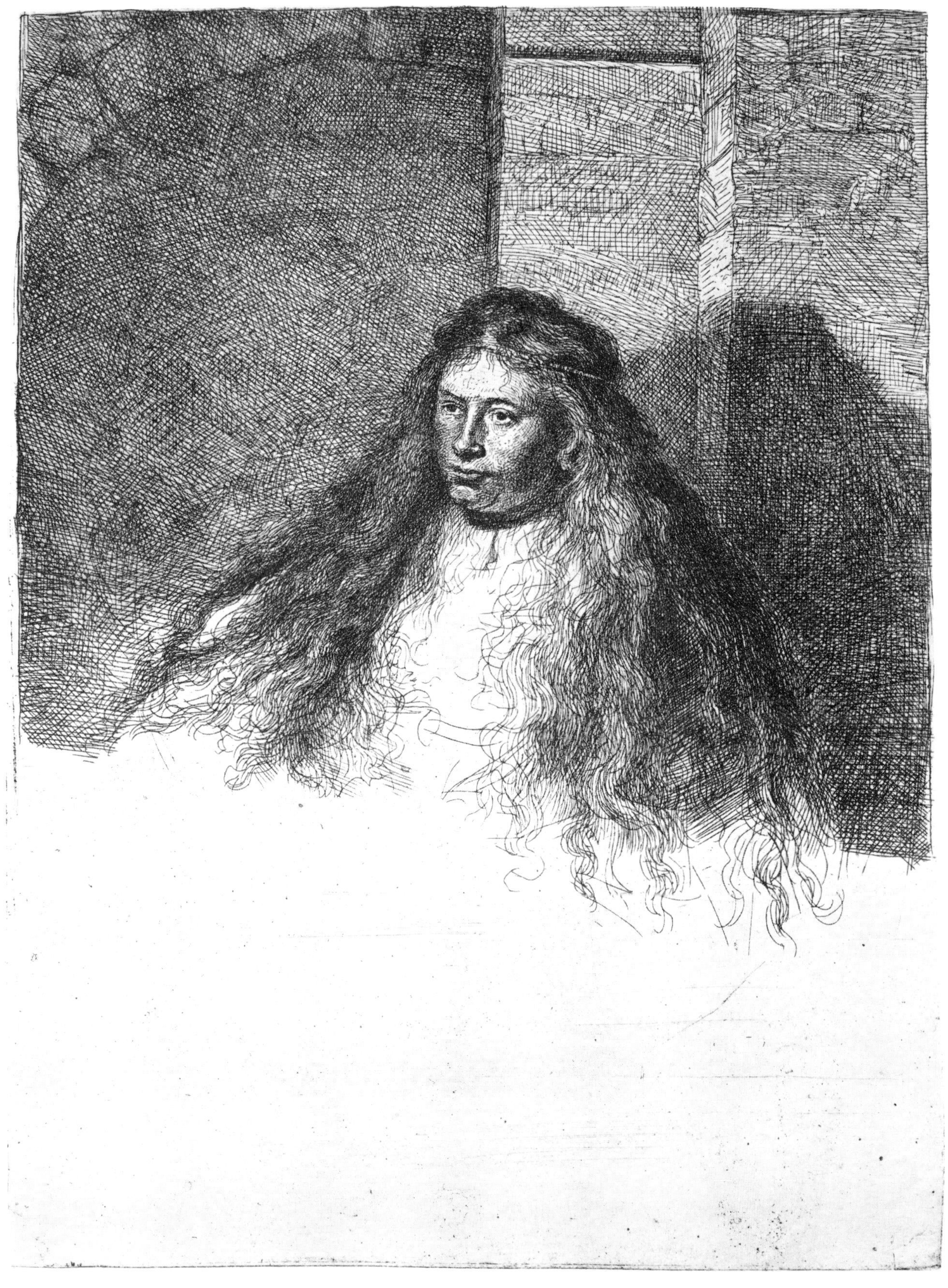

The great Jewish bride. 1635.

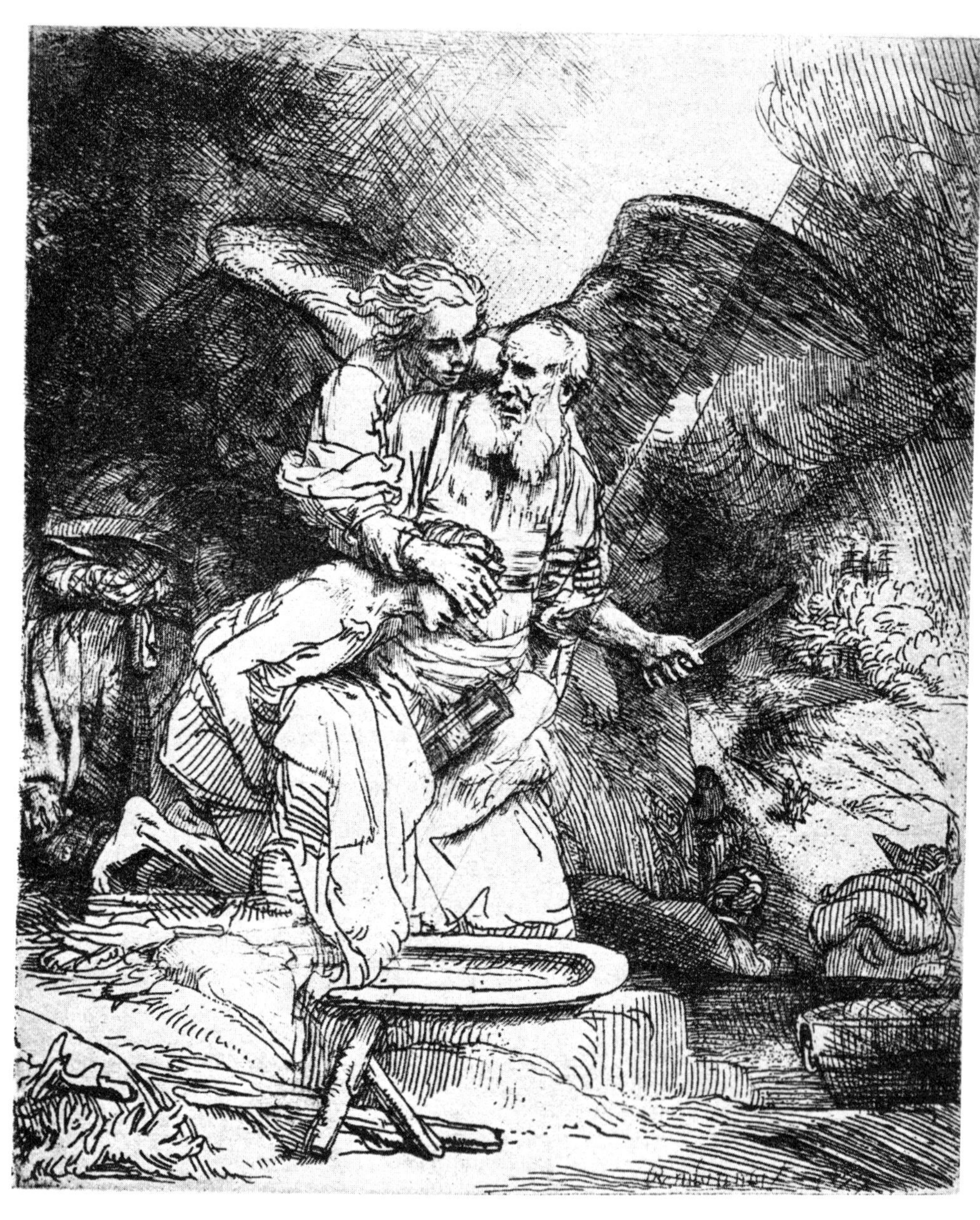

Abraham's sacrifice. 1655.

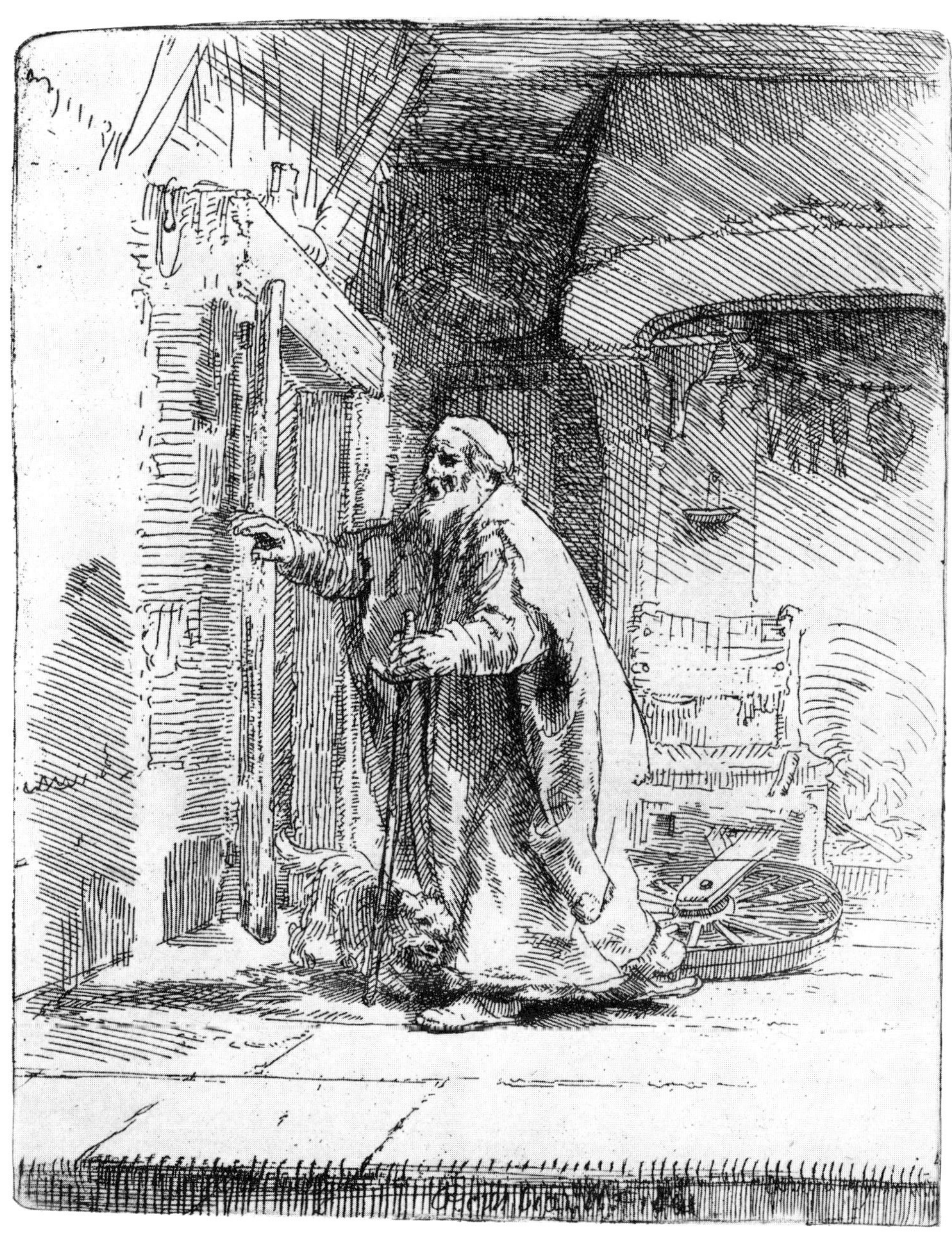

The blindness of Tobit. 1651.

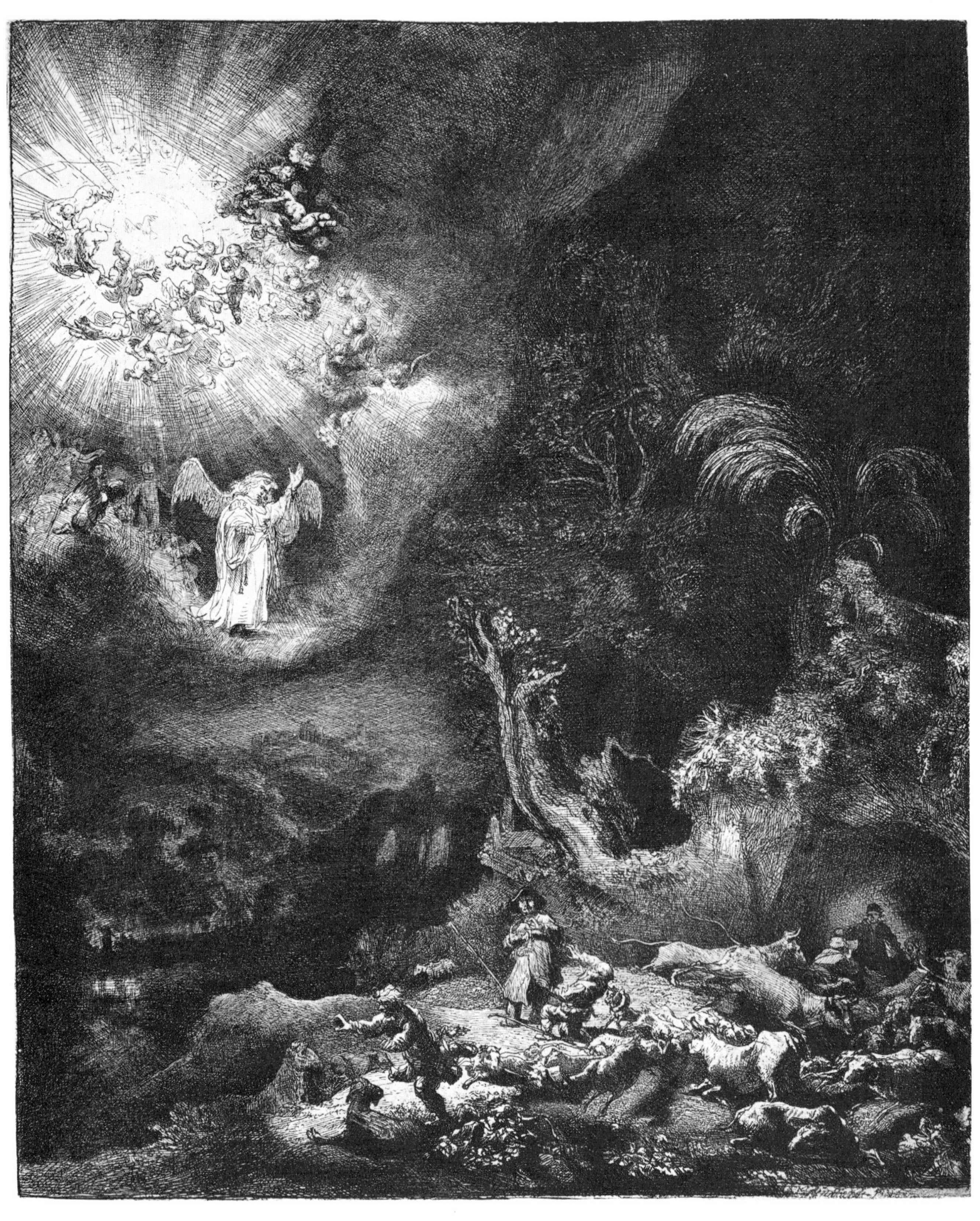

The angel appearing to the shepherds. 1634.

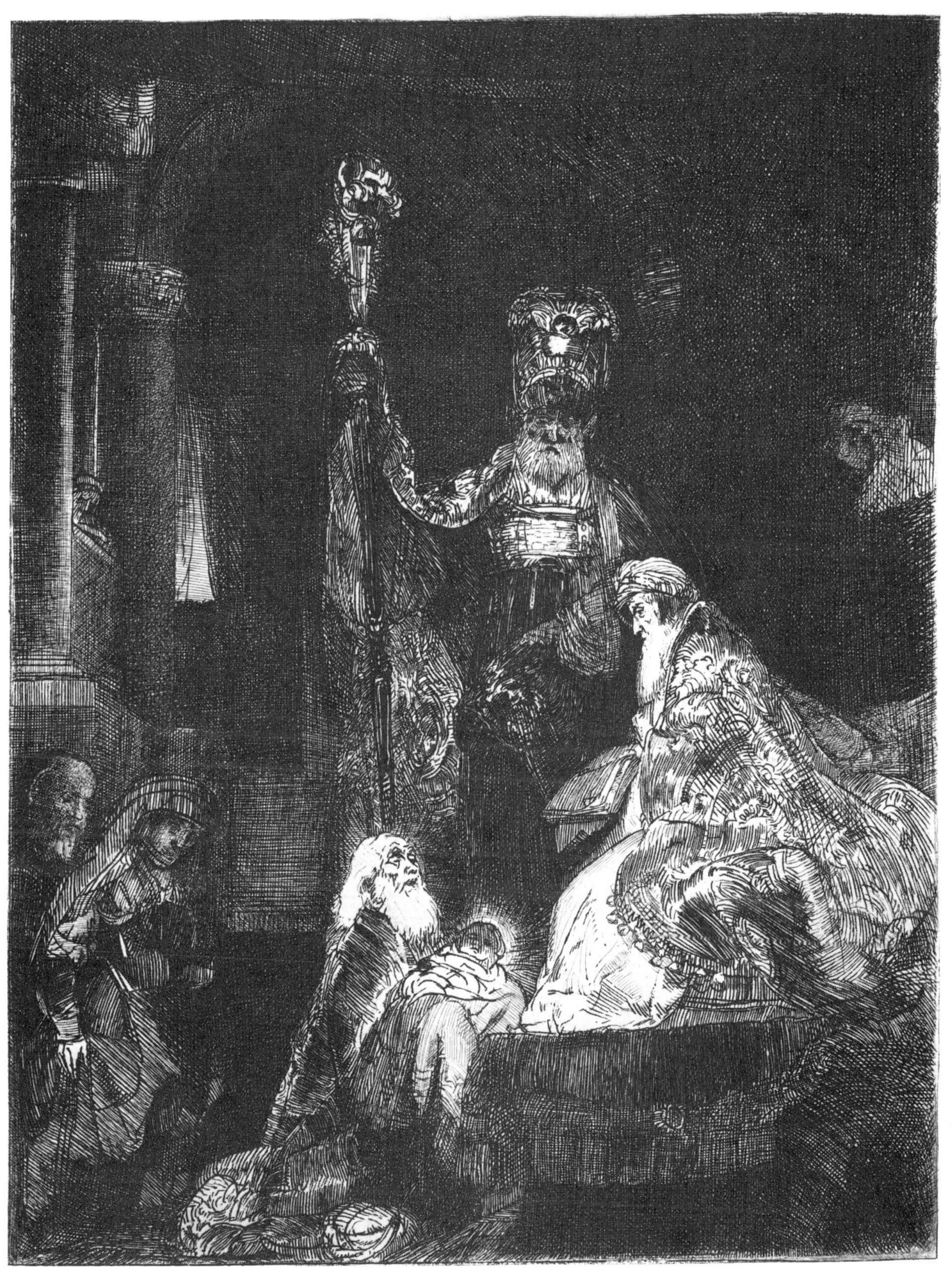

The Presentation in the Temple. 1657(?).

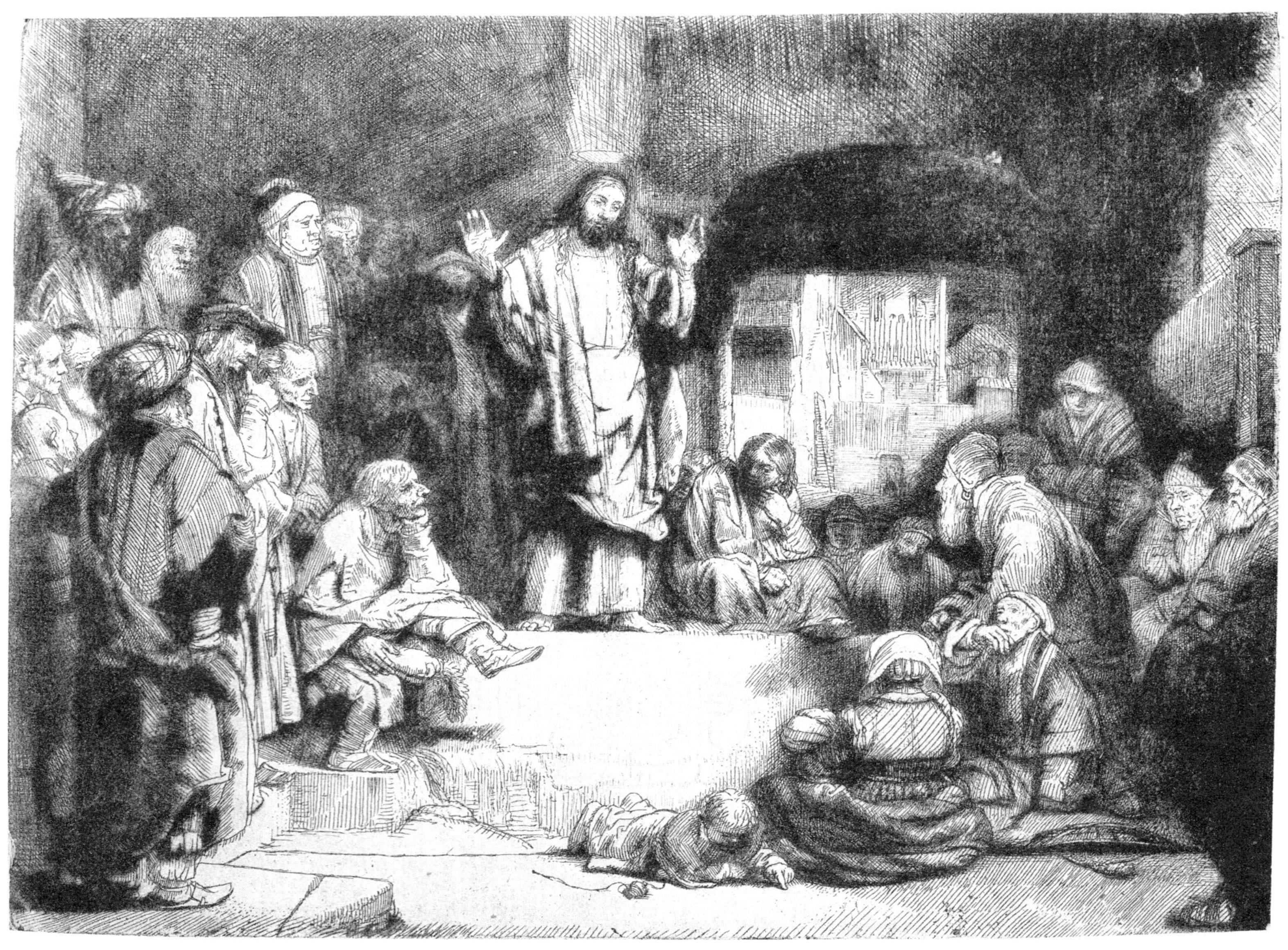

Christ preaching ("La Petite Tombe"). Ca. 1635.

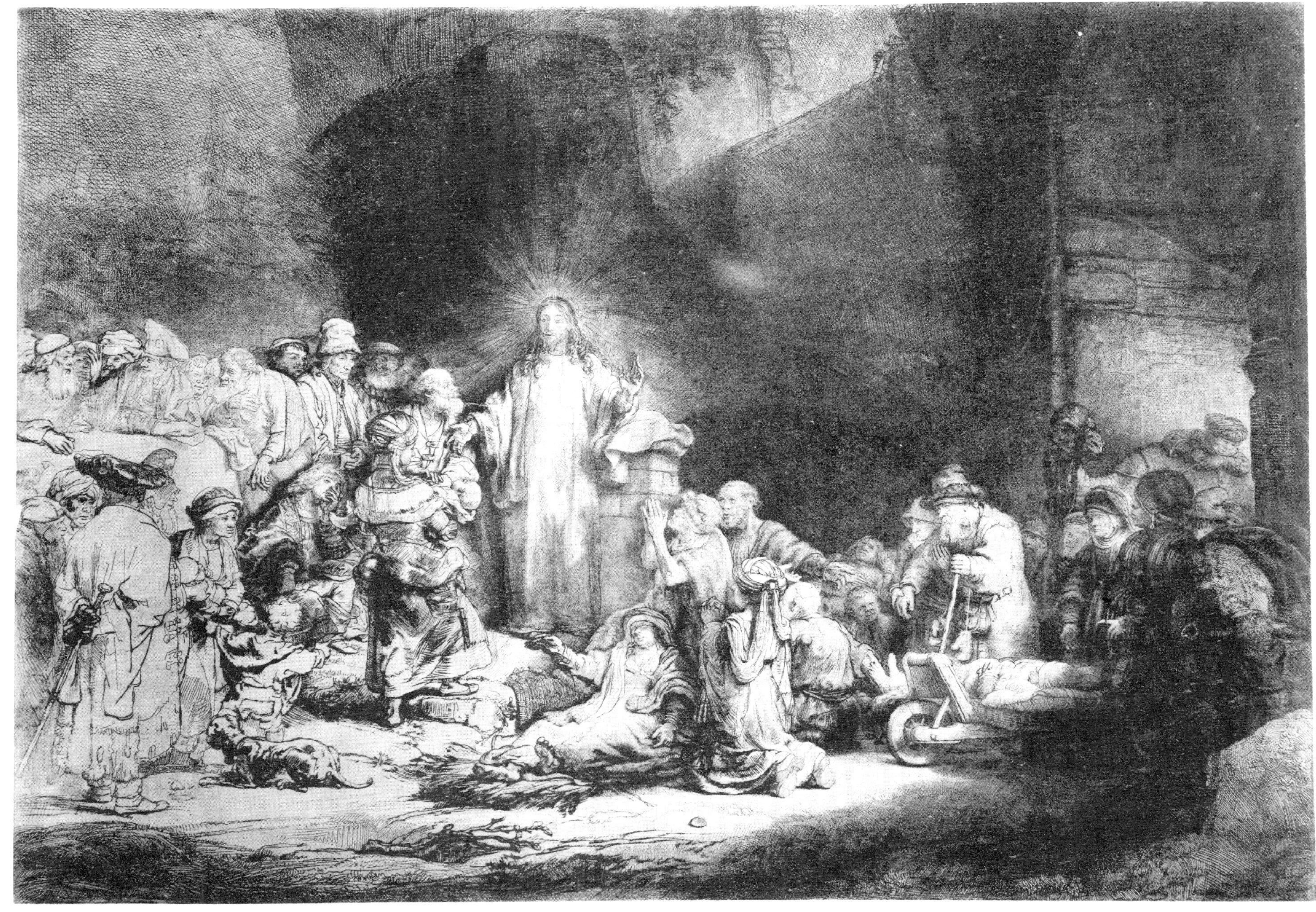

Christ healing the sick (the "Hundred-Guilder Print"). 1649(?).

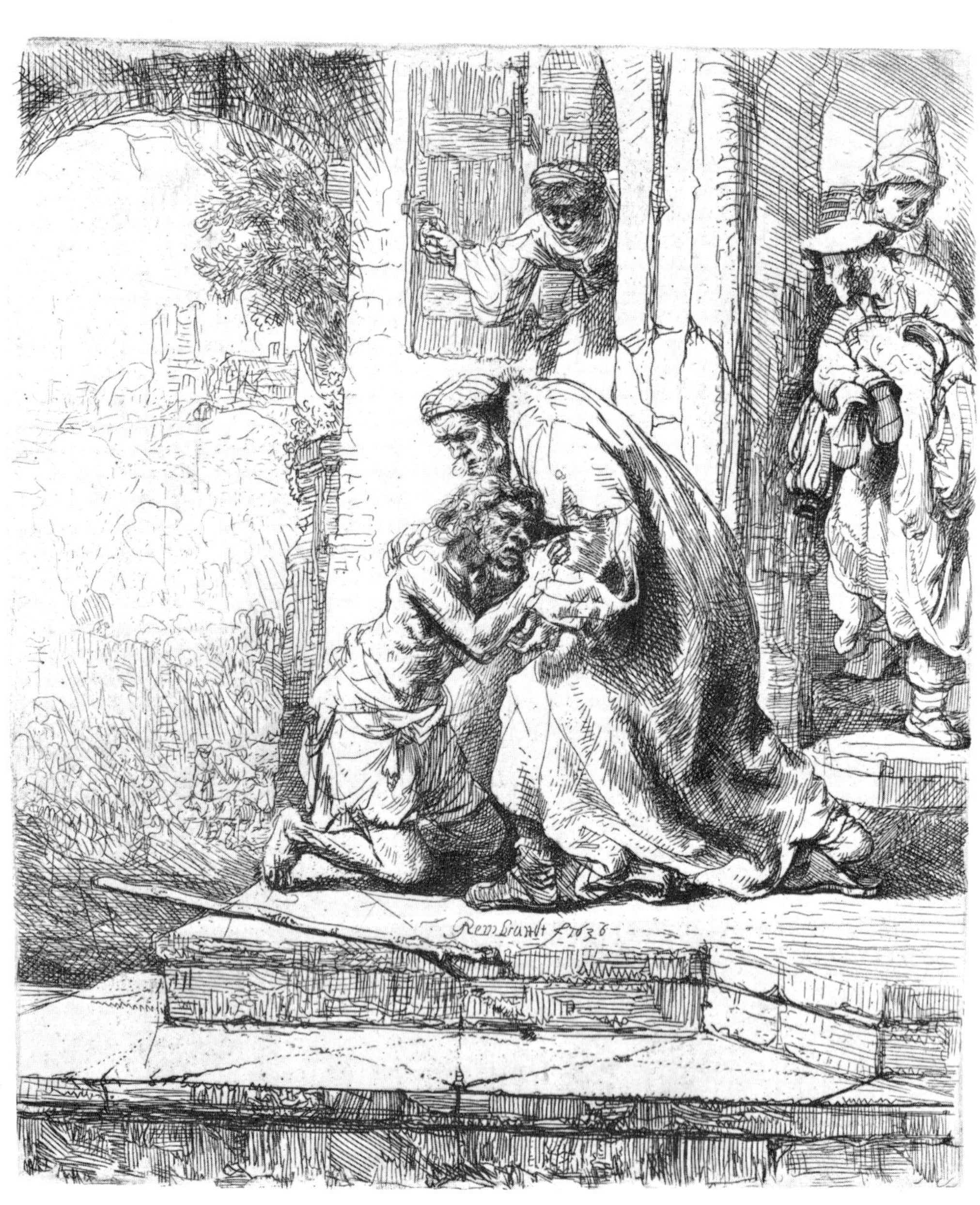

The return of the Prodigal Son. 1636.

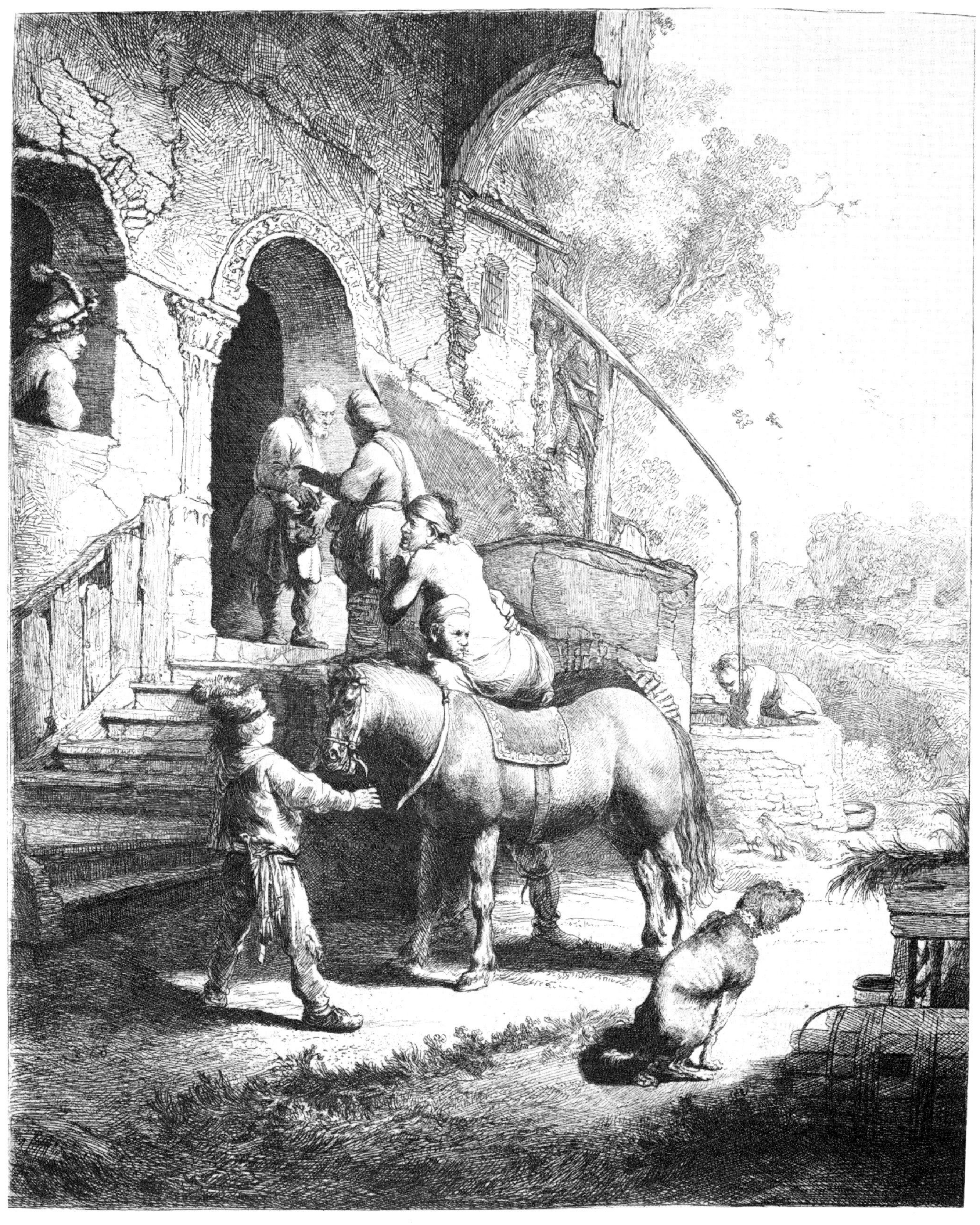

The good Samaritan. 1633.

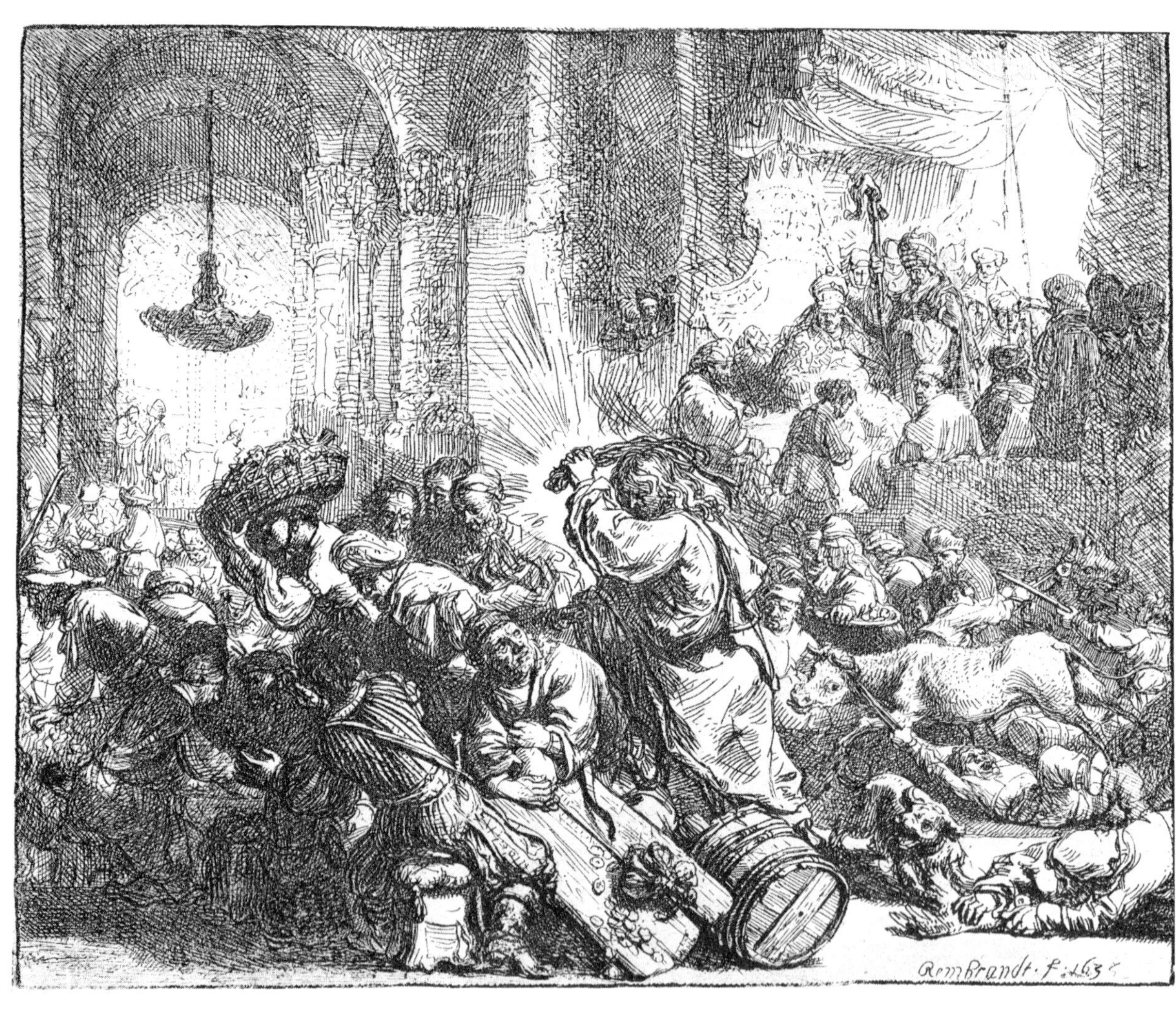

Christ driving the money changers from the Temple. 1635.

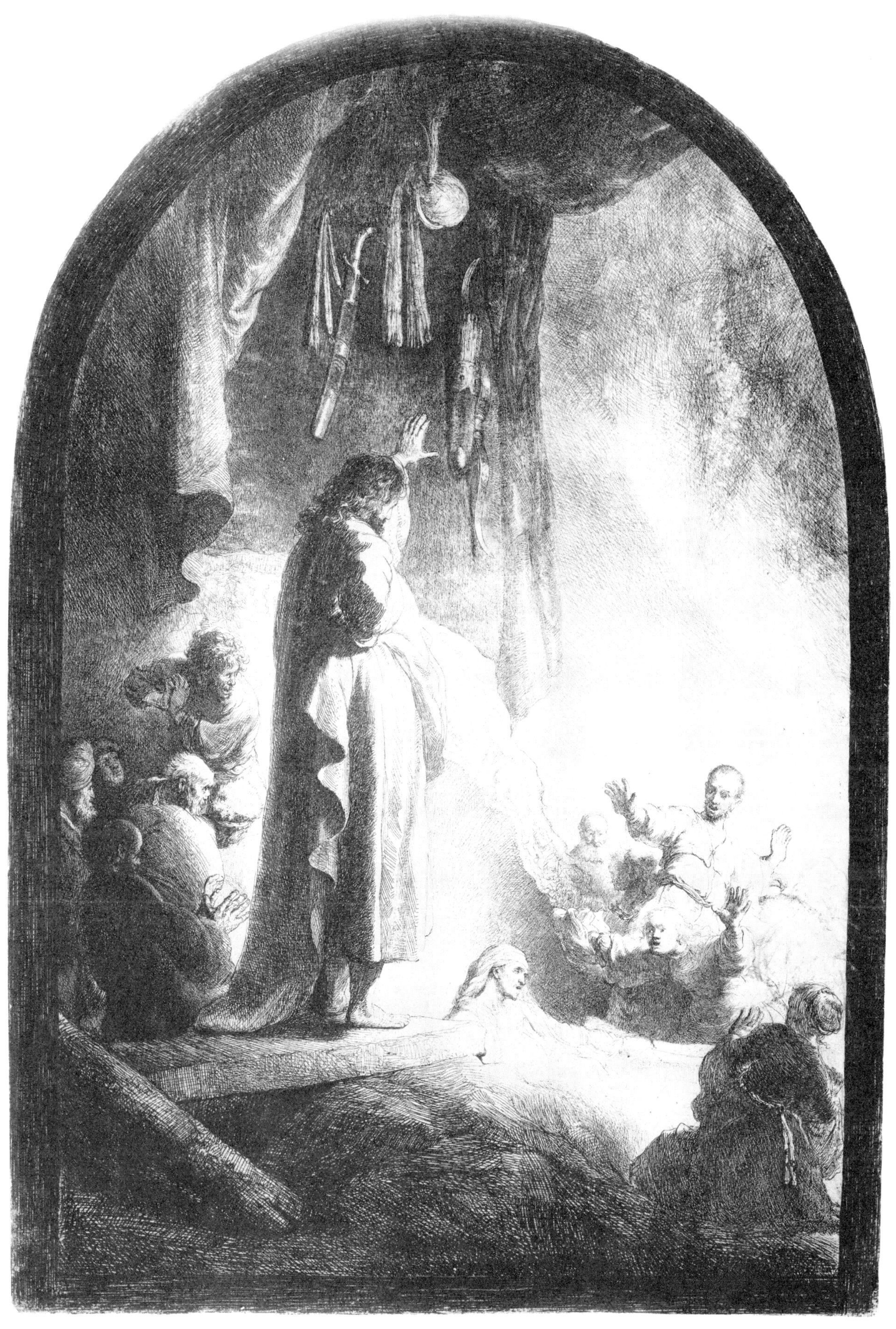

The Raising of Lazarus. 1632.

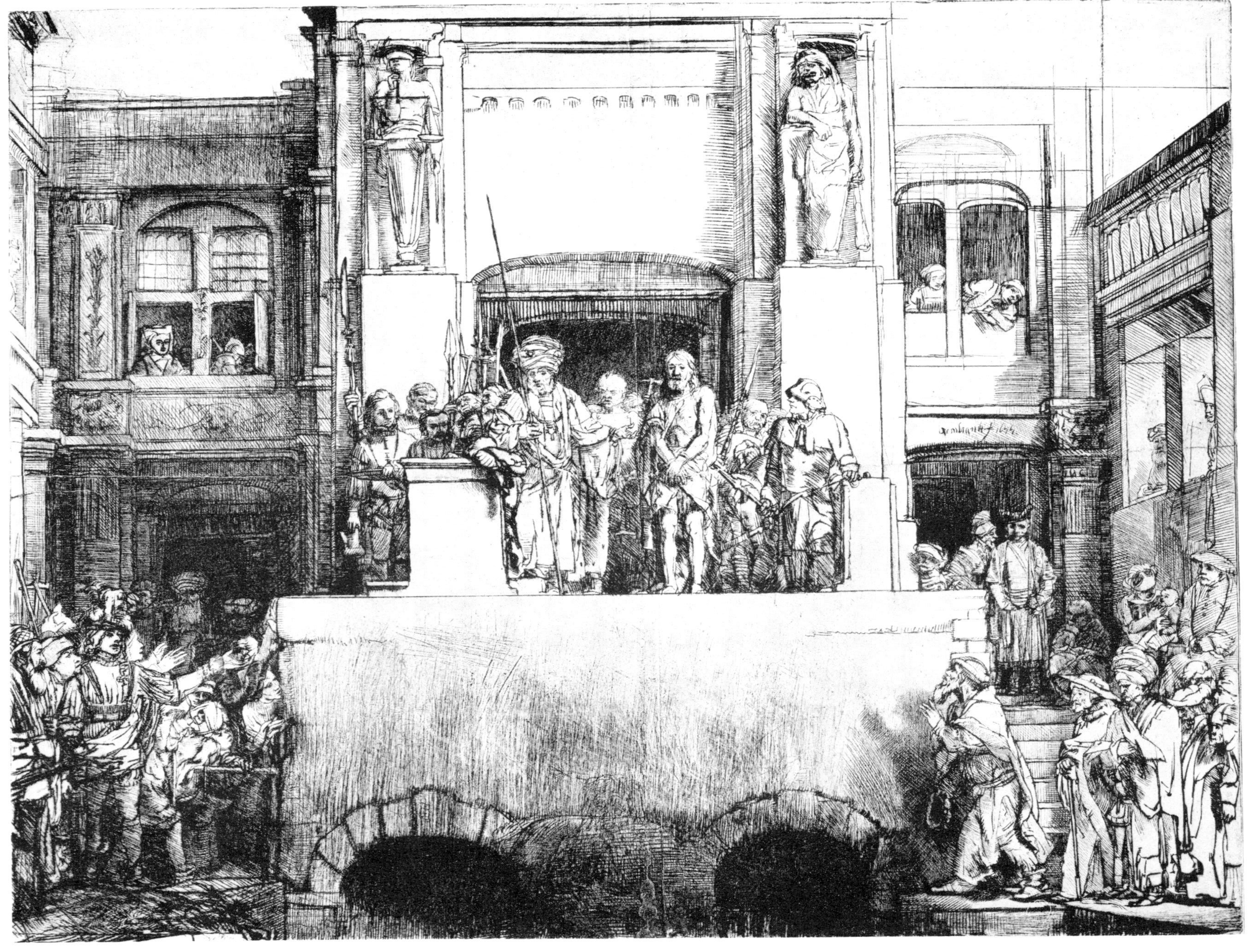

Christ presented to the people. 1655.

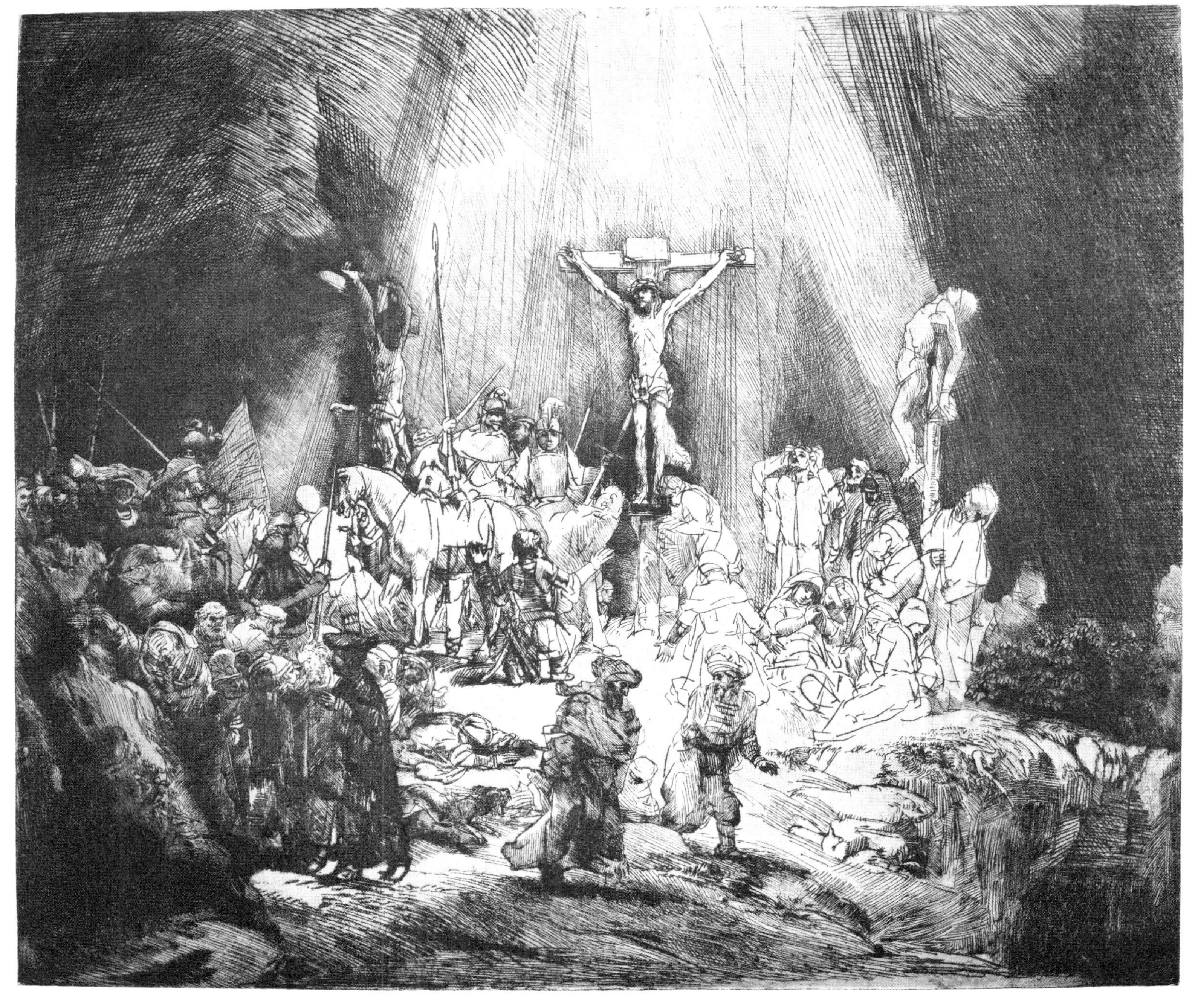

The three crosses. 1653.

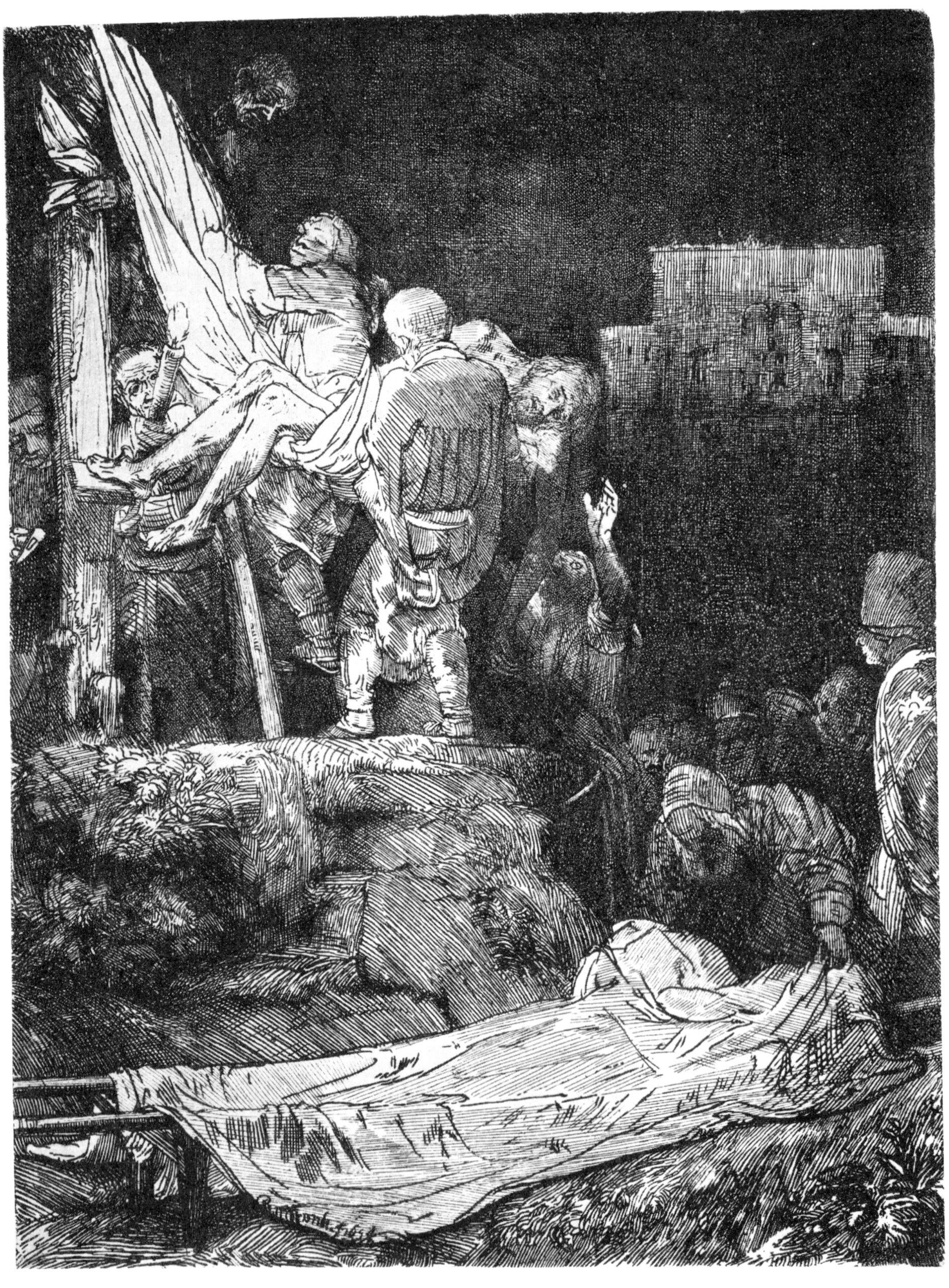

The descent from the Cross by torchlight. 1654.

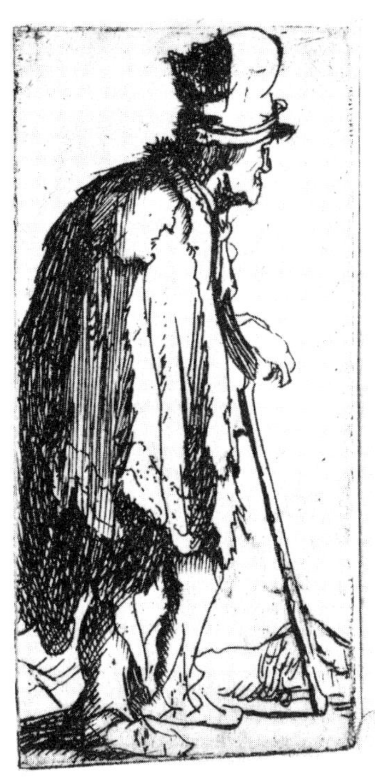

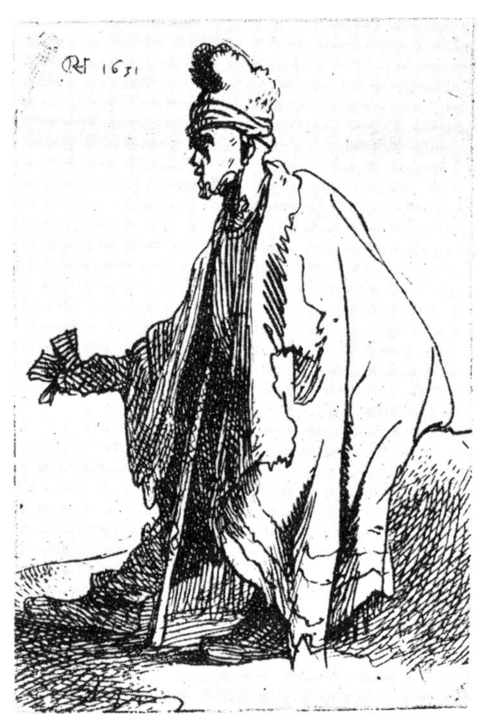

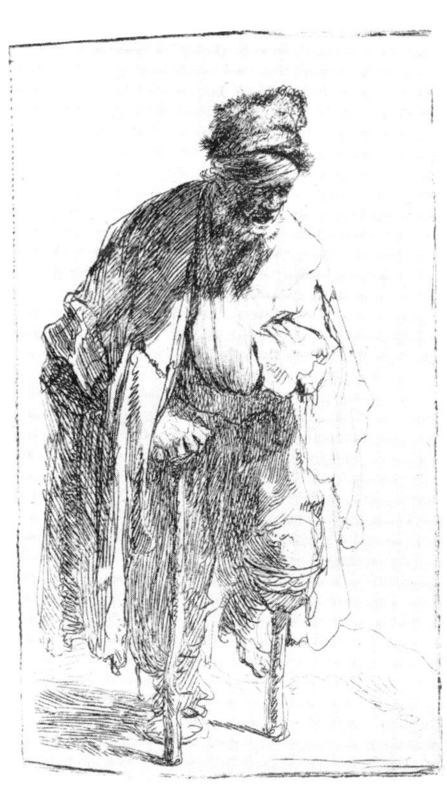

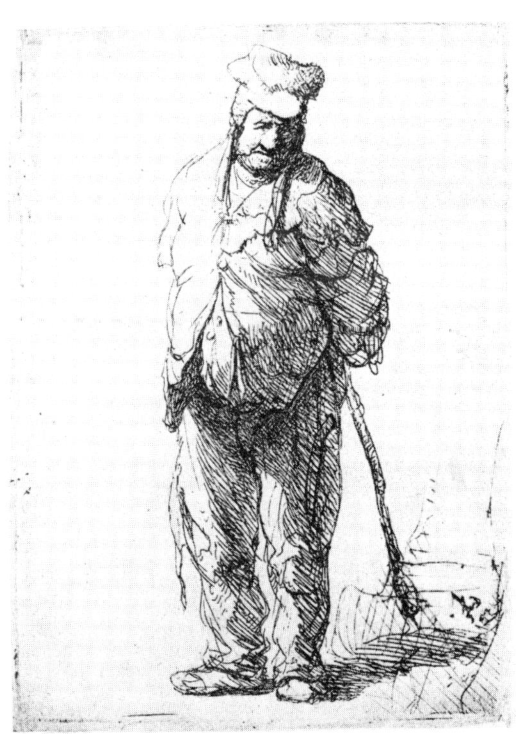

Top, left: Beggar with crippled hands leaning on a stick. 1630(?).
Top, right: The leper (Lazarus Klep). 1631. *Bottom, left:* Beggar with a wooden leg. 1630(?). *Bottom, right:* Peasant with his hands behind him. 1630(?).

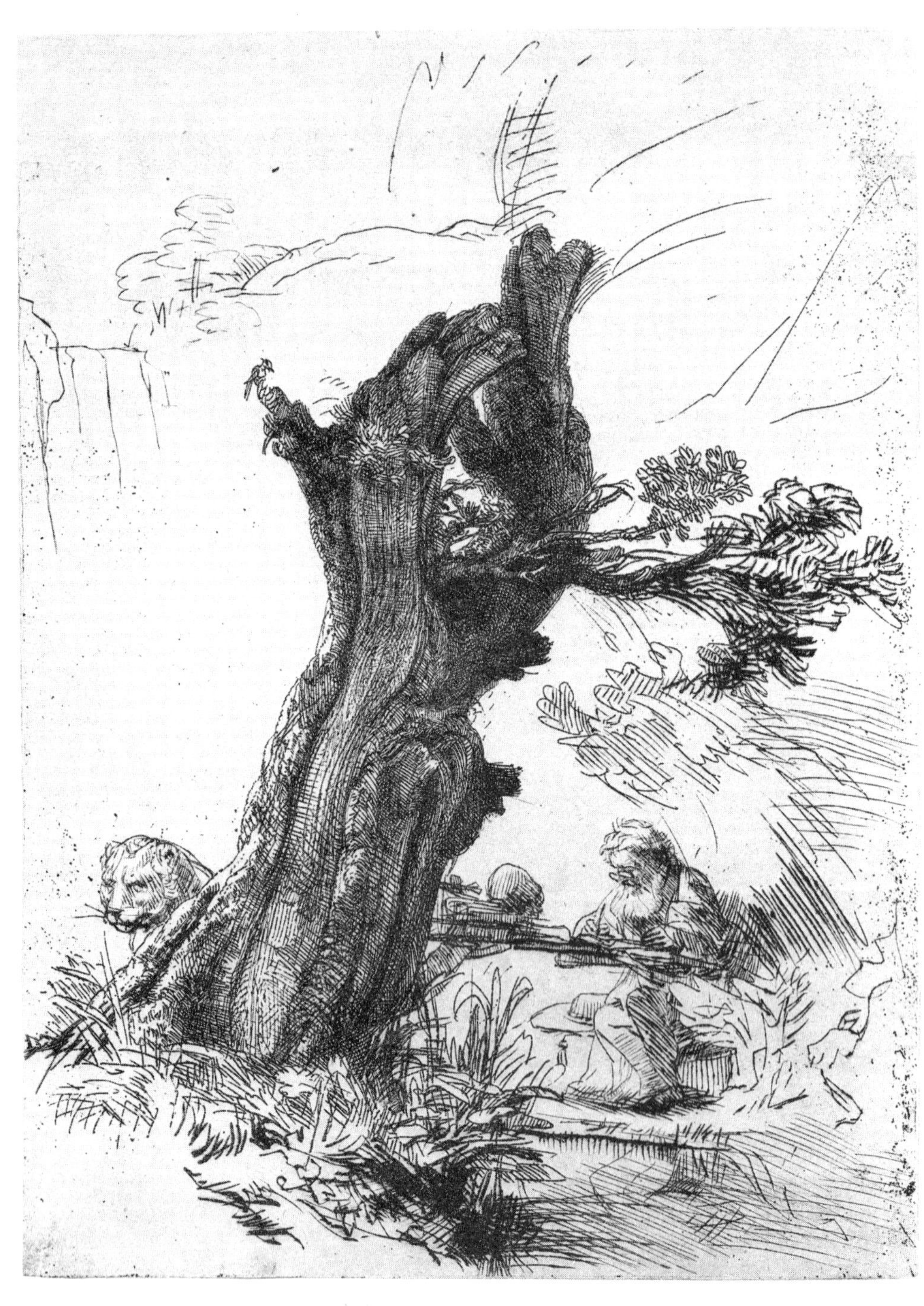

St. Jerome beside a pollard willow. 1648.

St. Francis beneath a tree, praying. 1657.

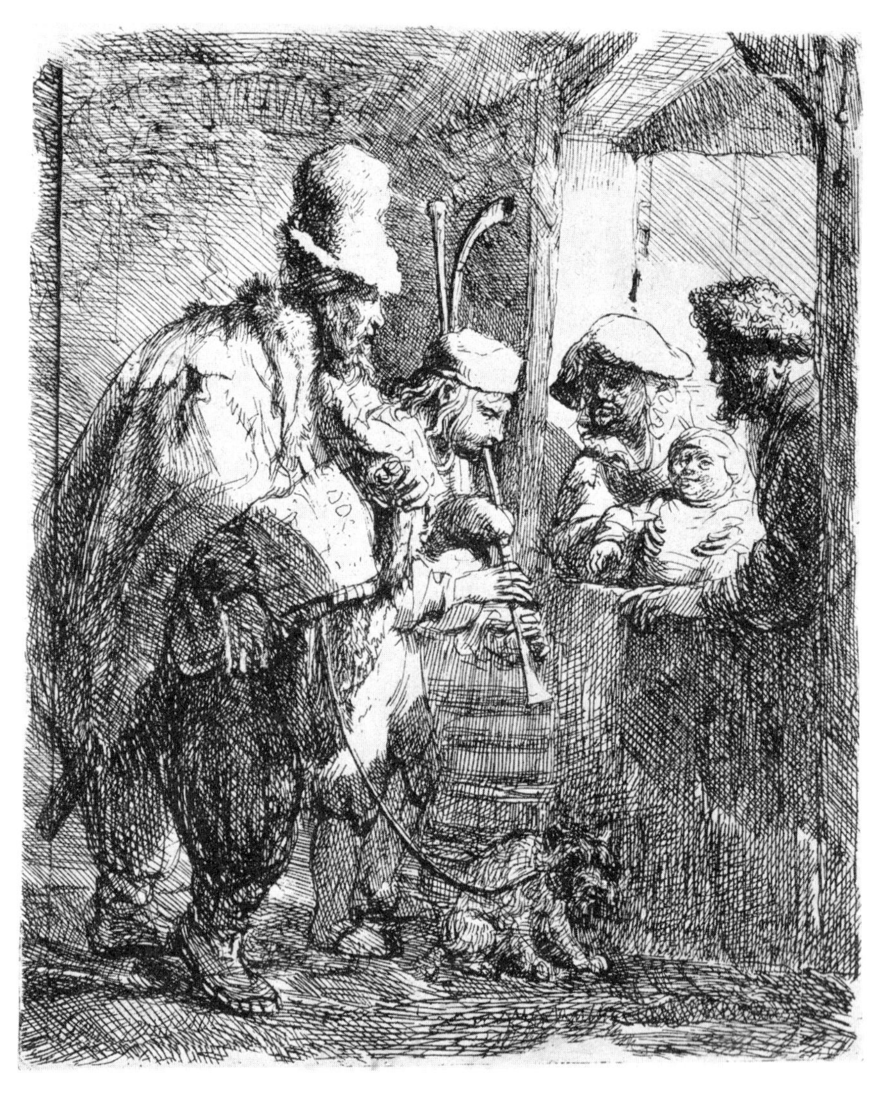

The strolling musicians. 1635(?).

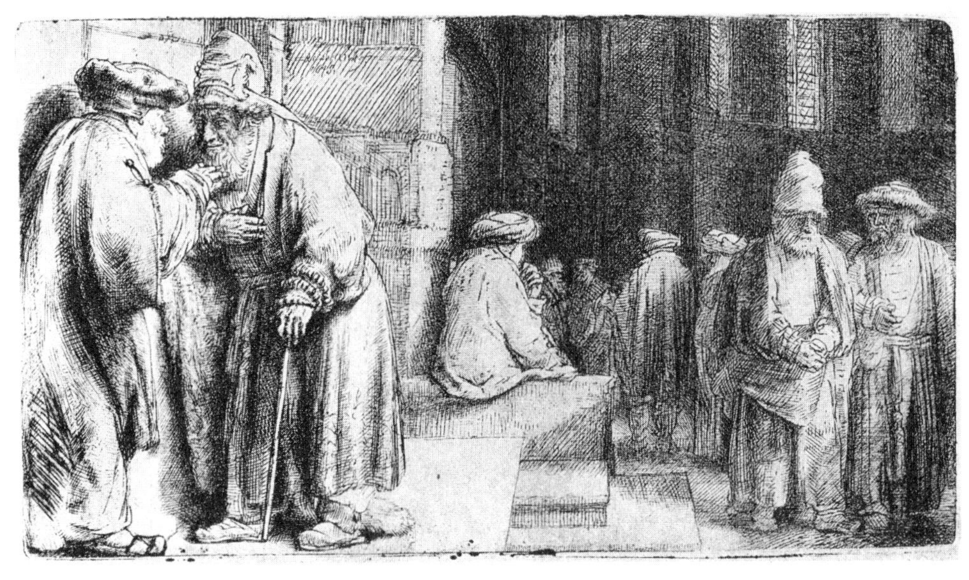

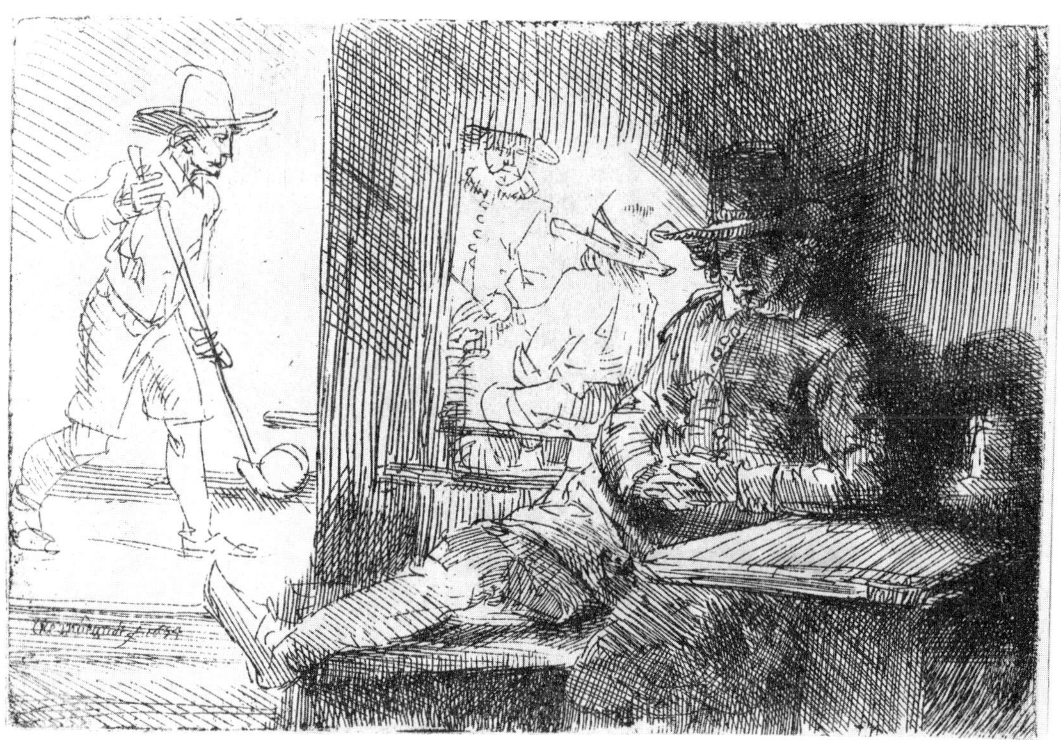

Top: Jews in synagogue. 1648. *Bottom:* The golf player. 1654.

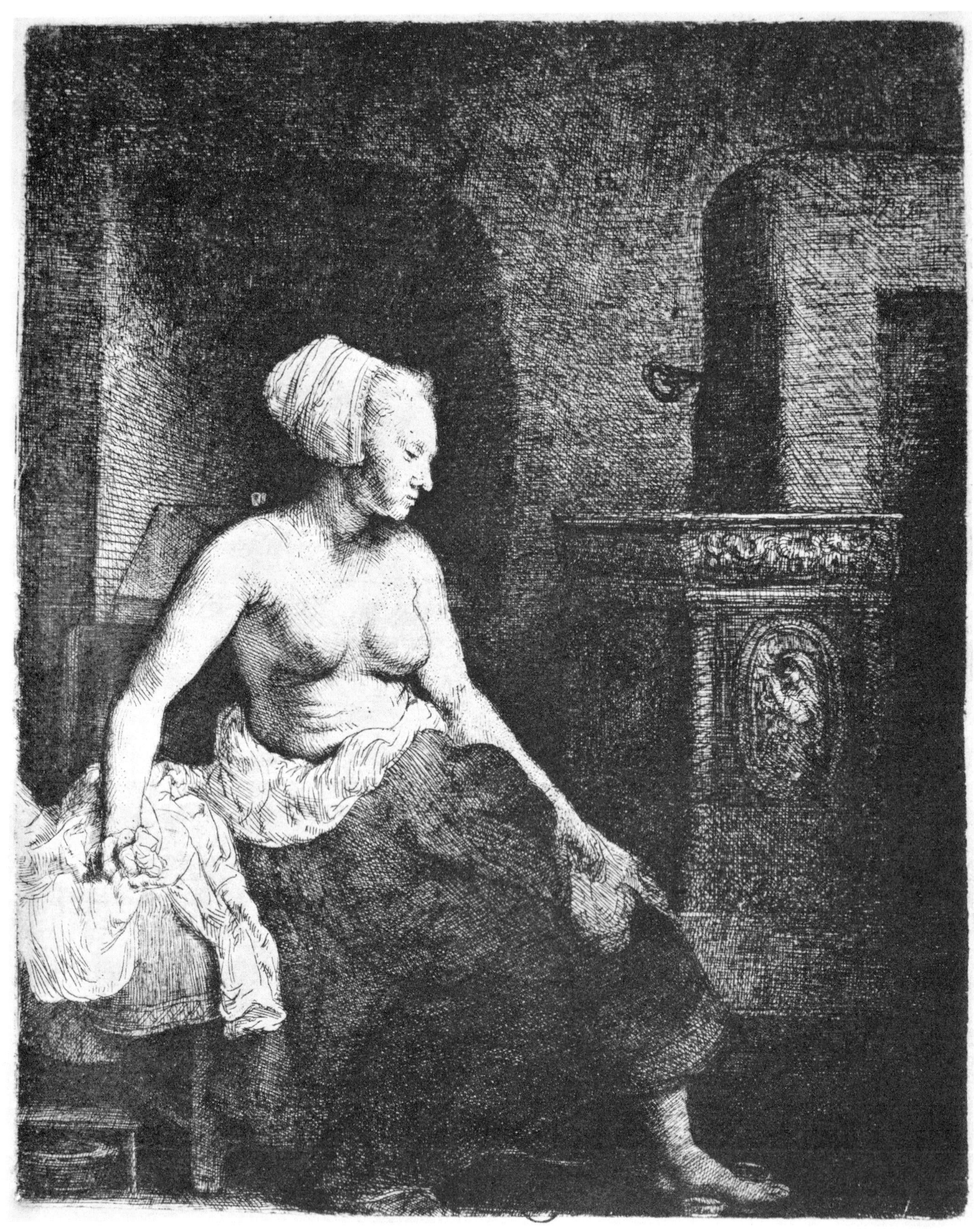

Woman sitting half-dressed beside a stove. 1658.

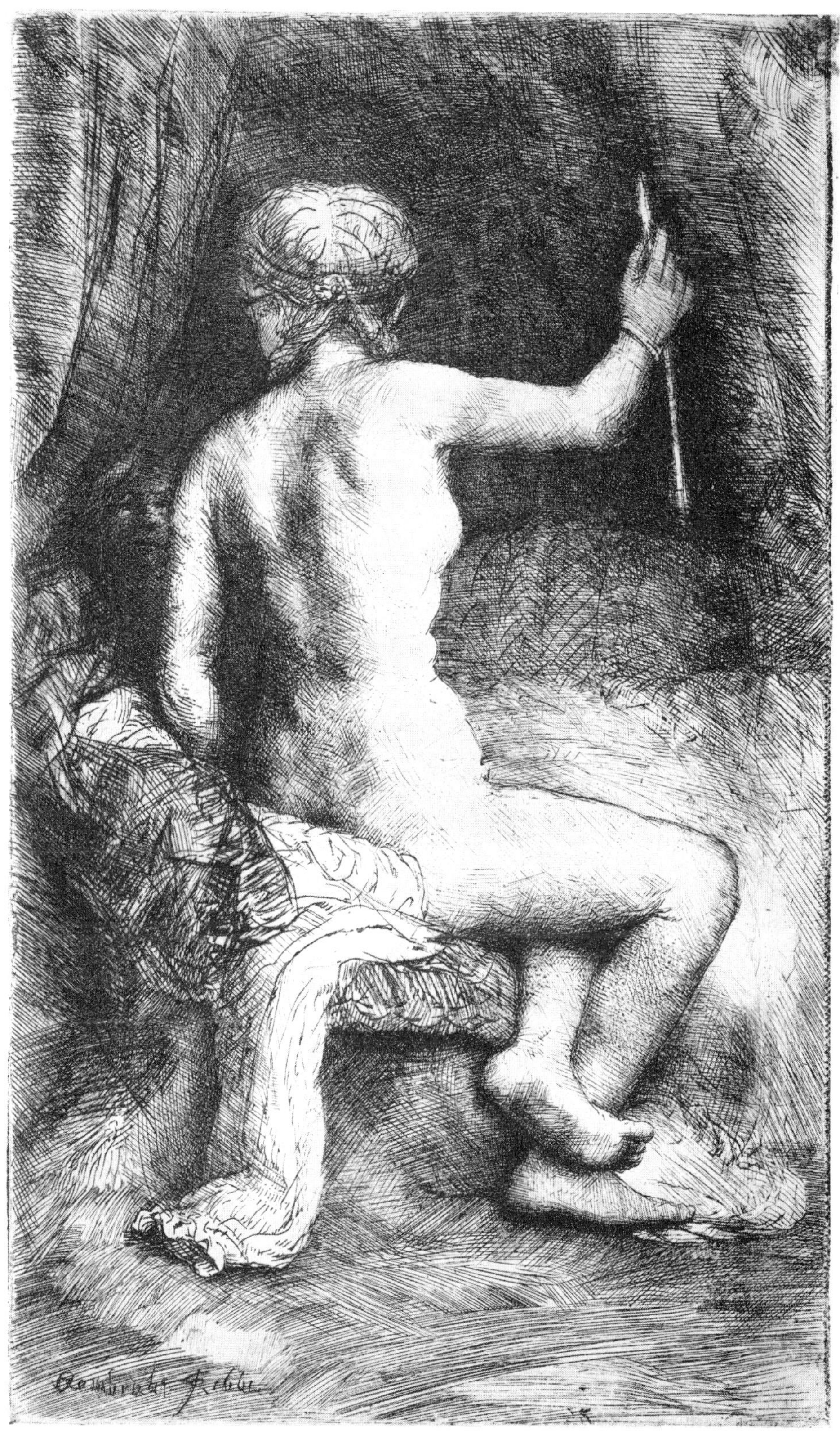

The woman with the arrow. 1661.

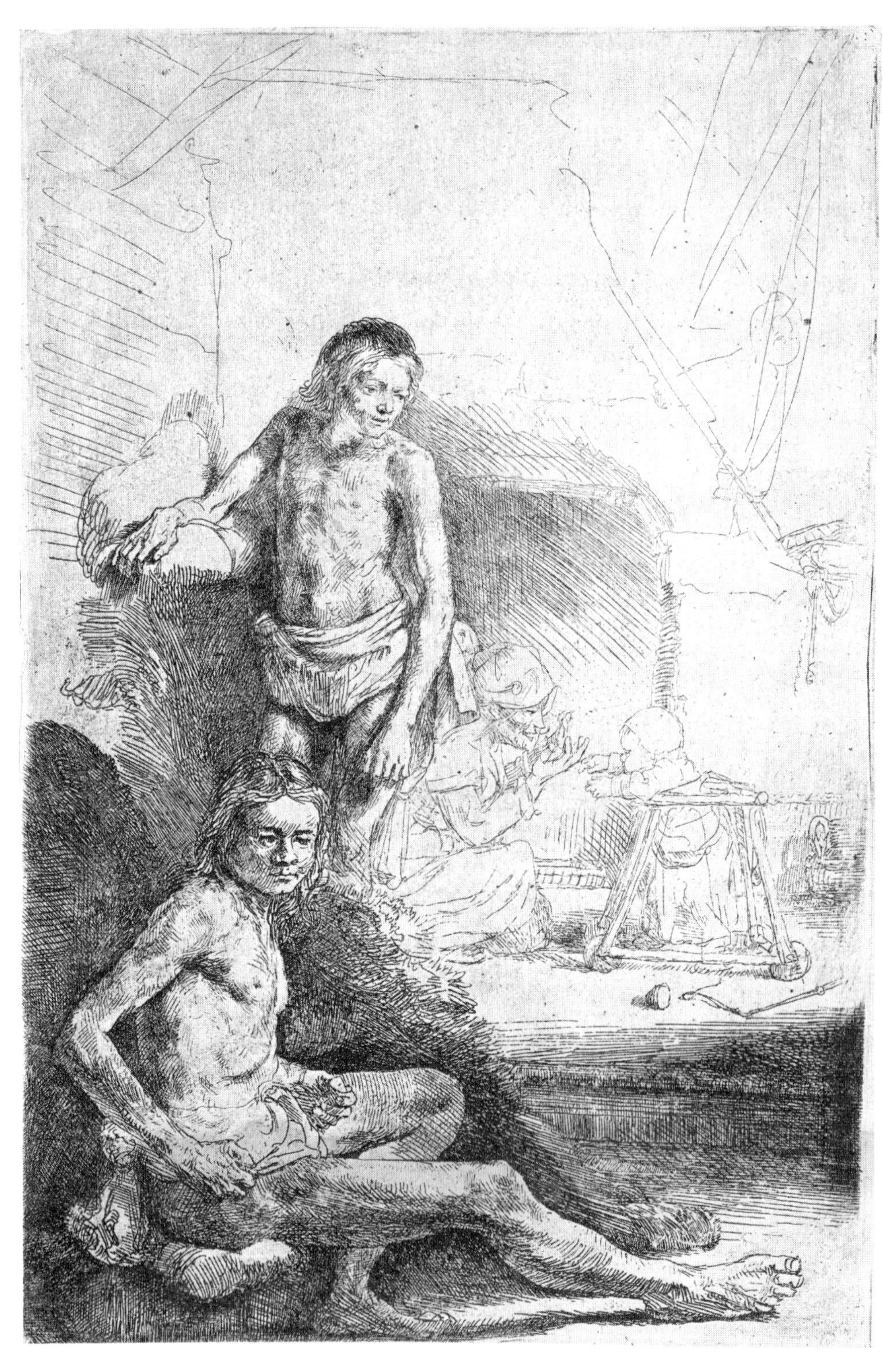

Nude man standing, another seated. 1646(?).

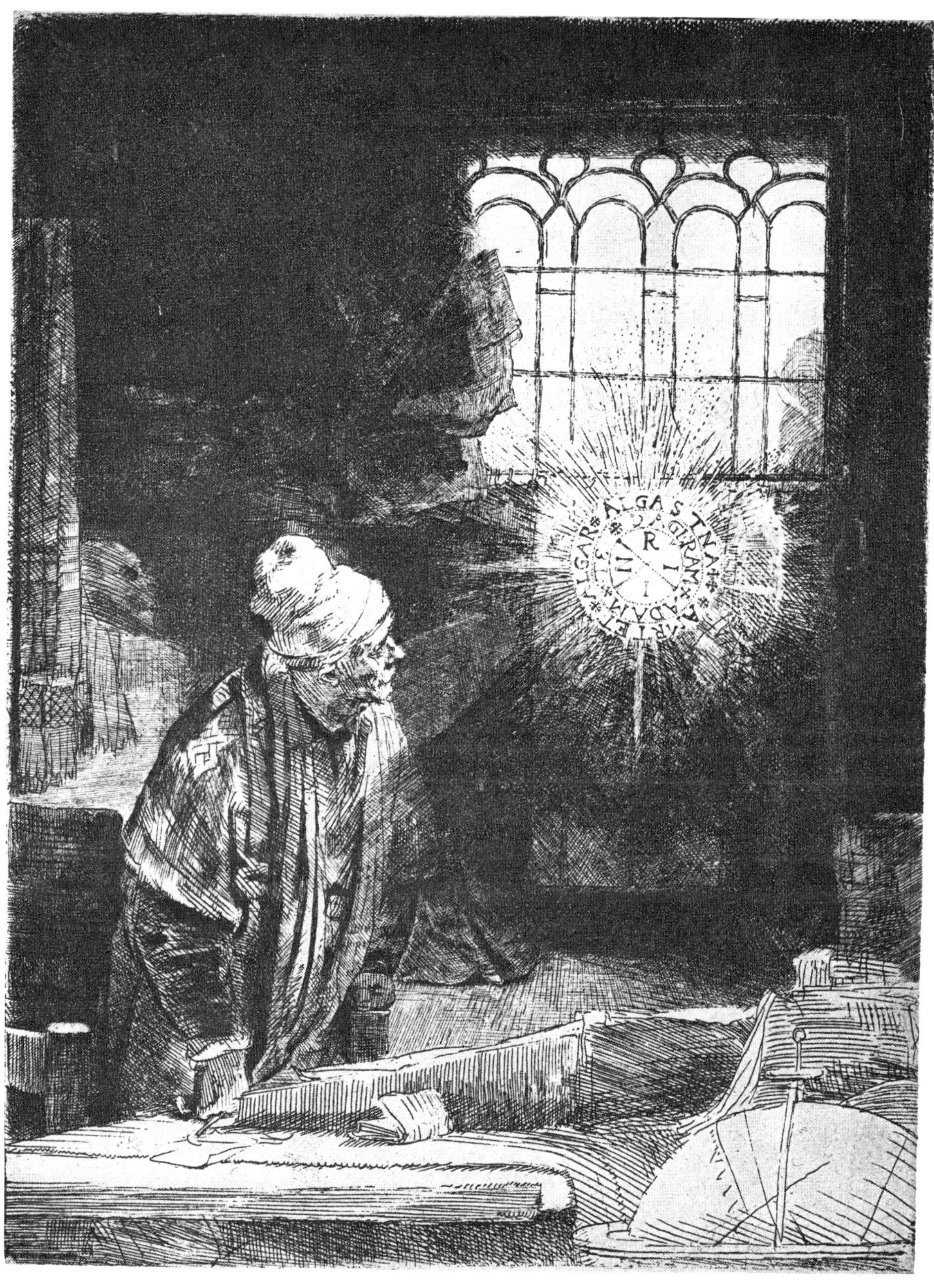

Faust in his study. 1652(?).

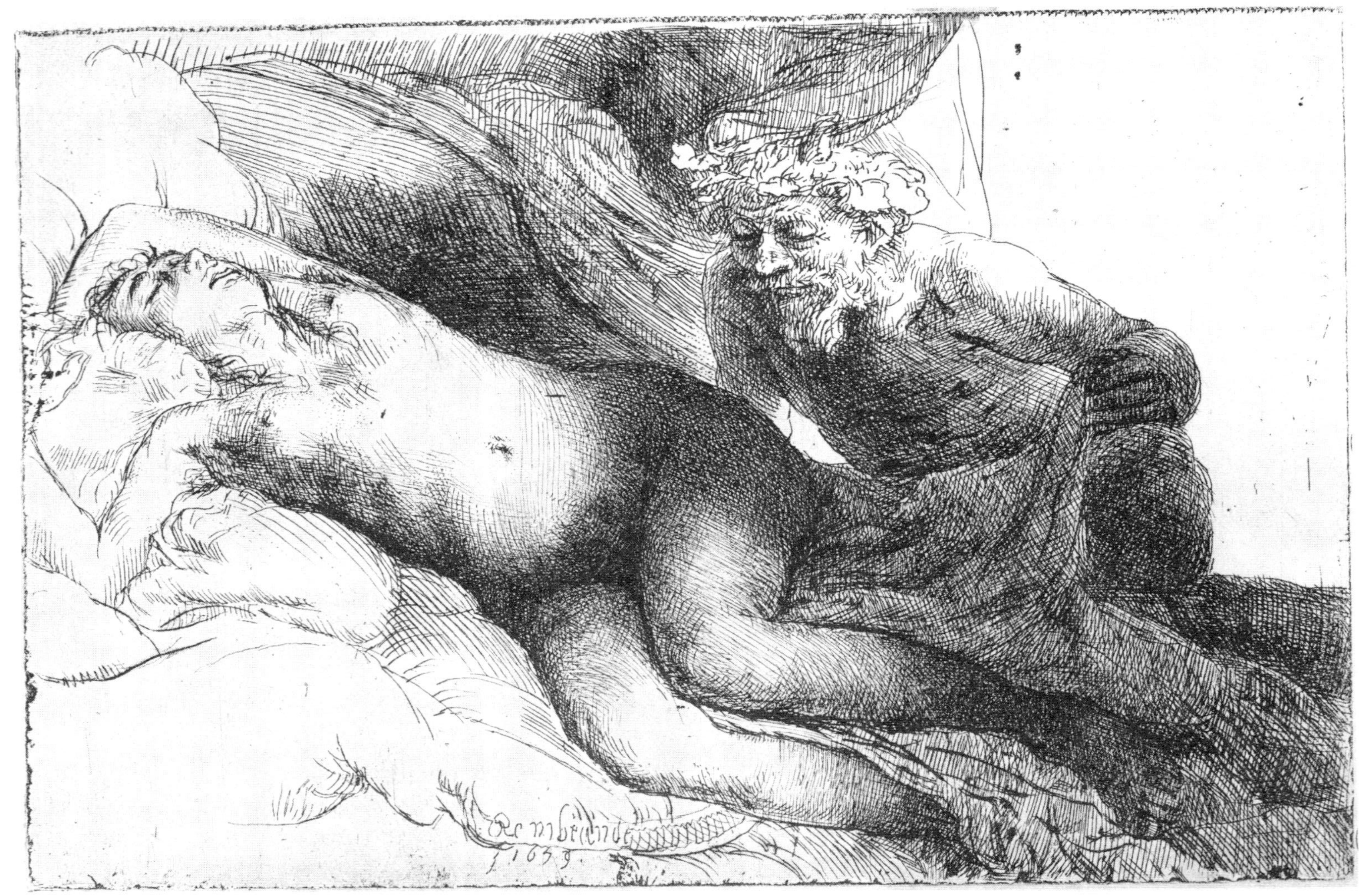

Jupiter and Antiope. 1659.

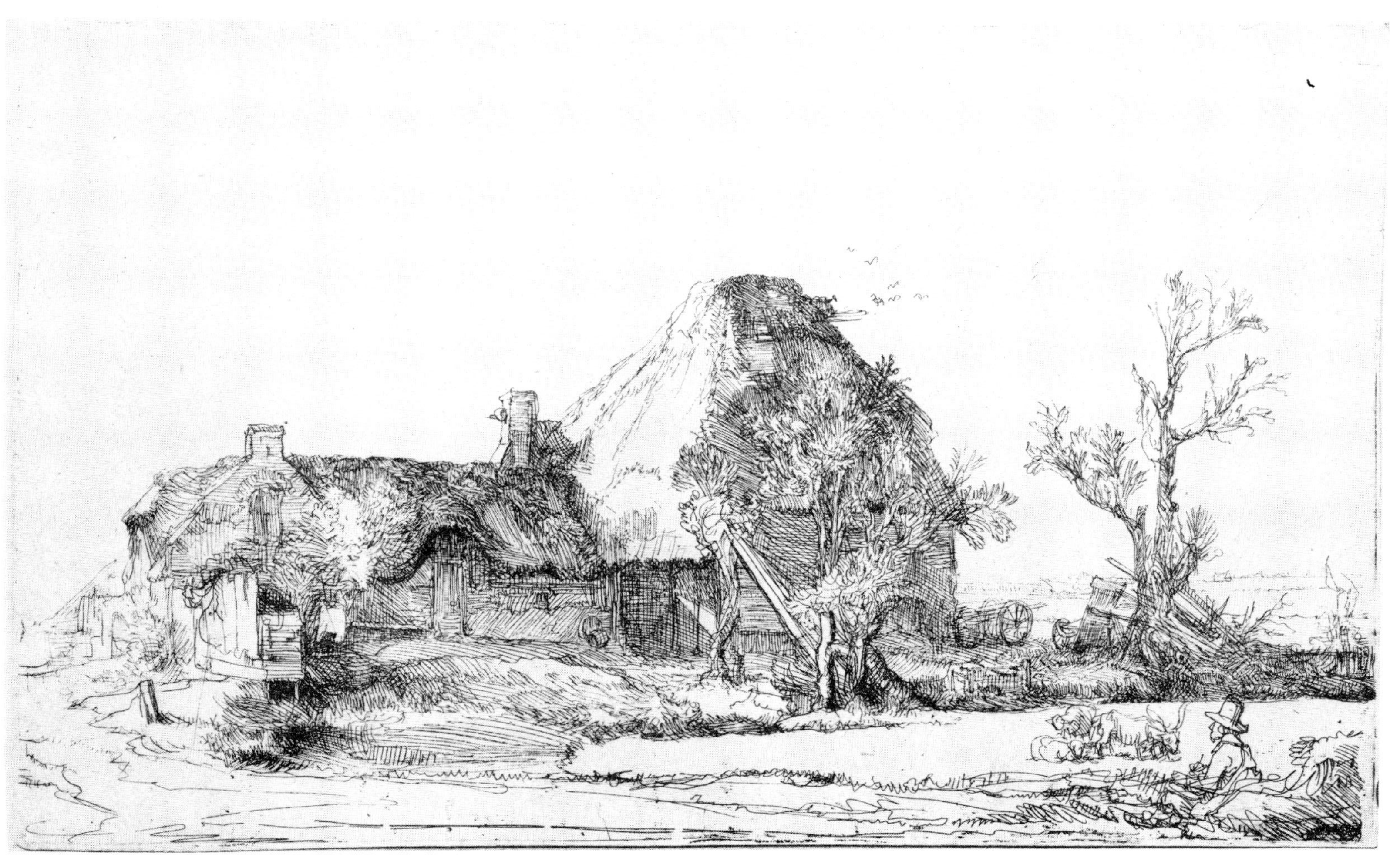

Landscape with farm buildings and a man sketching. 1645(?).

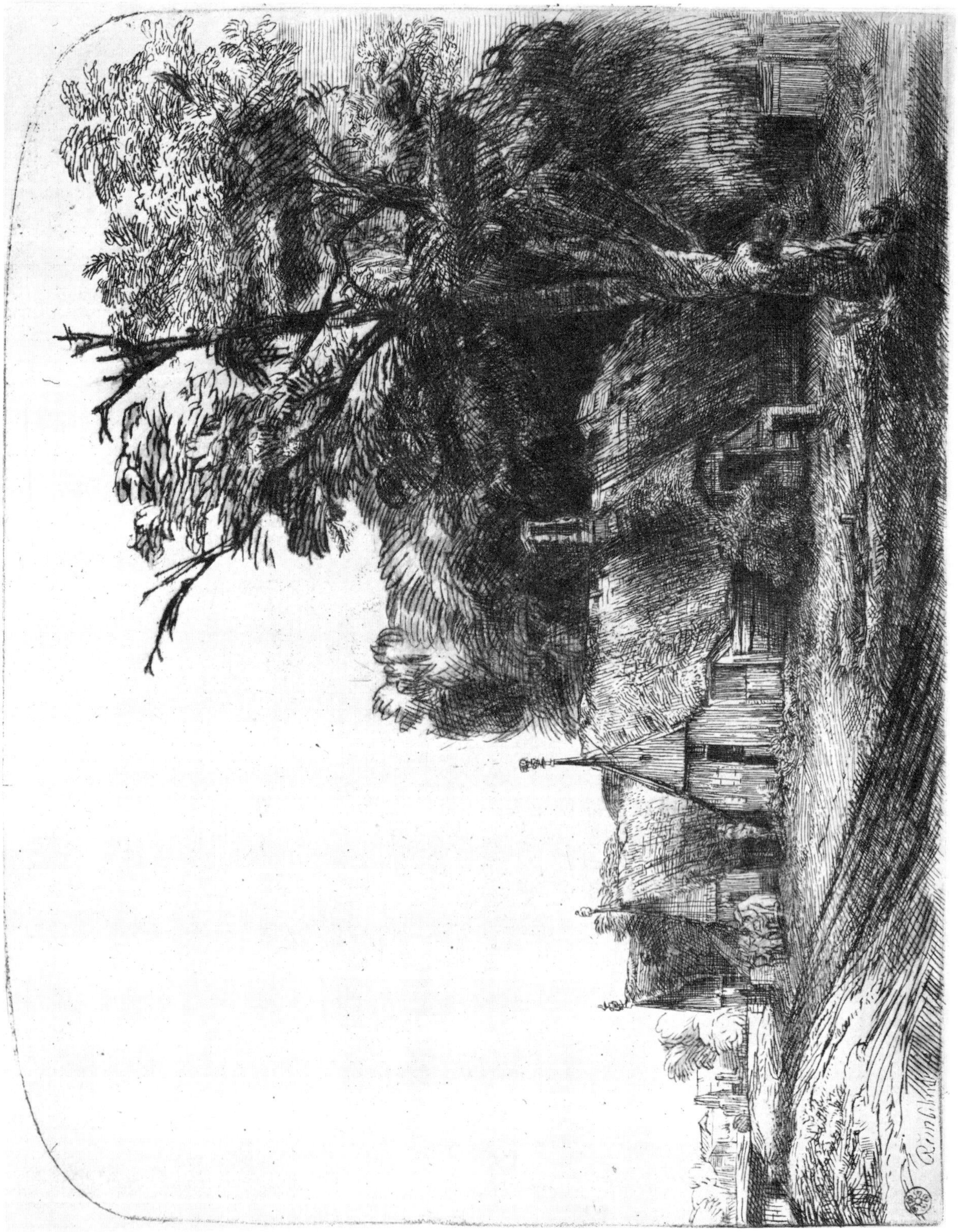

Three gabled cottages beside a road. 1650.

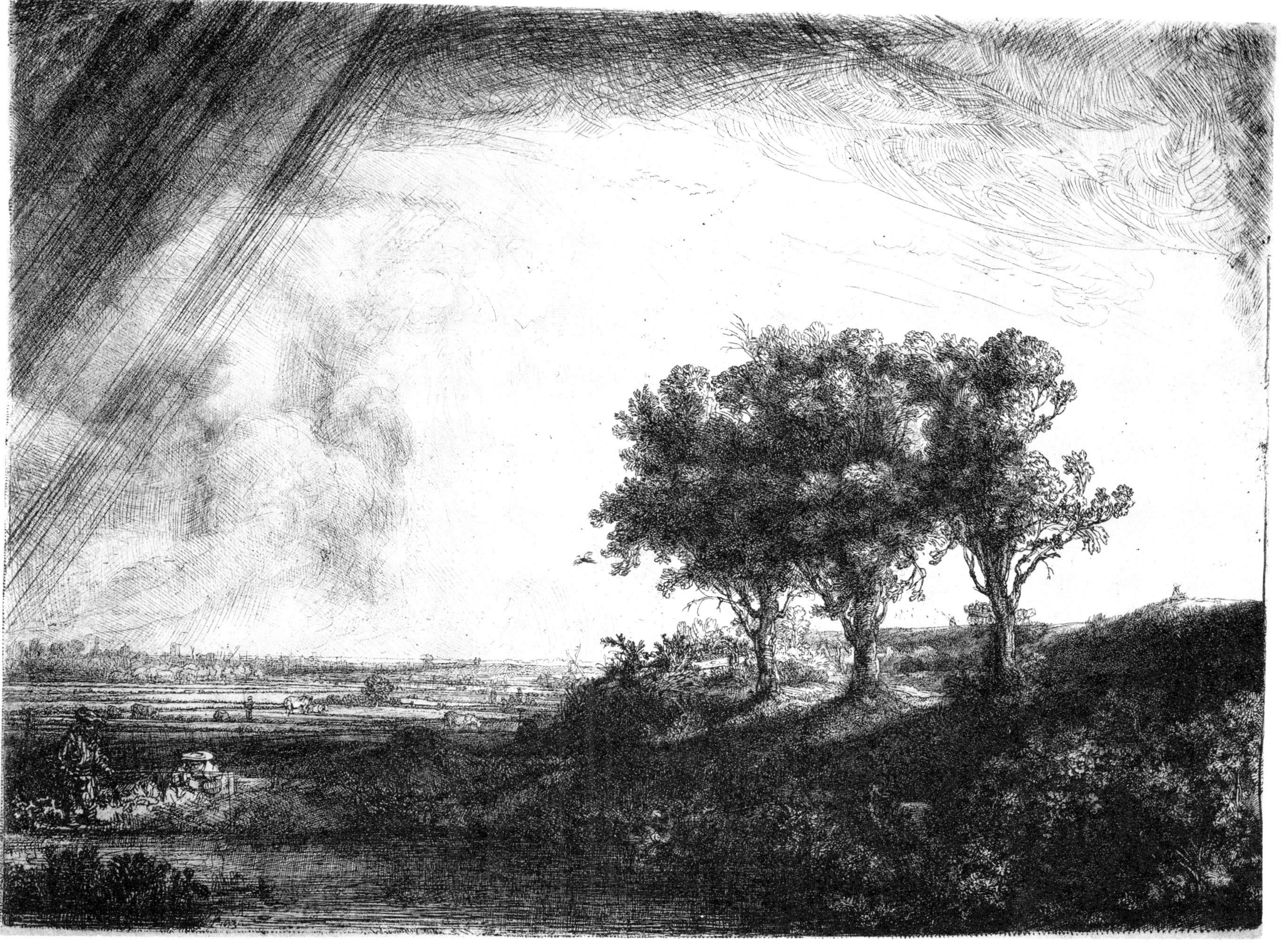

The three trees. 1643.

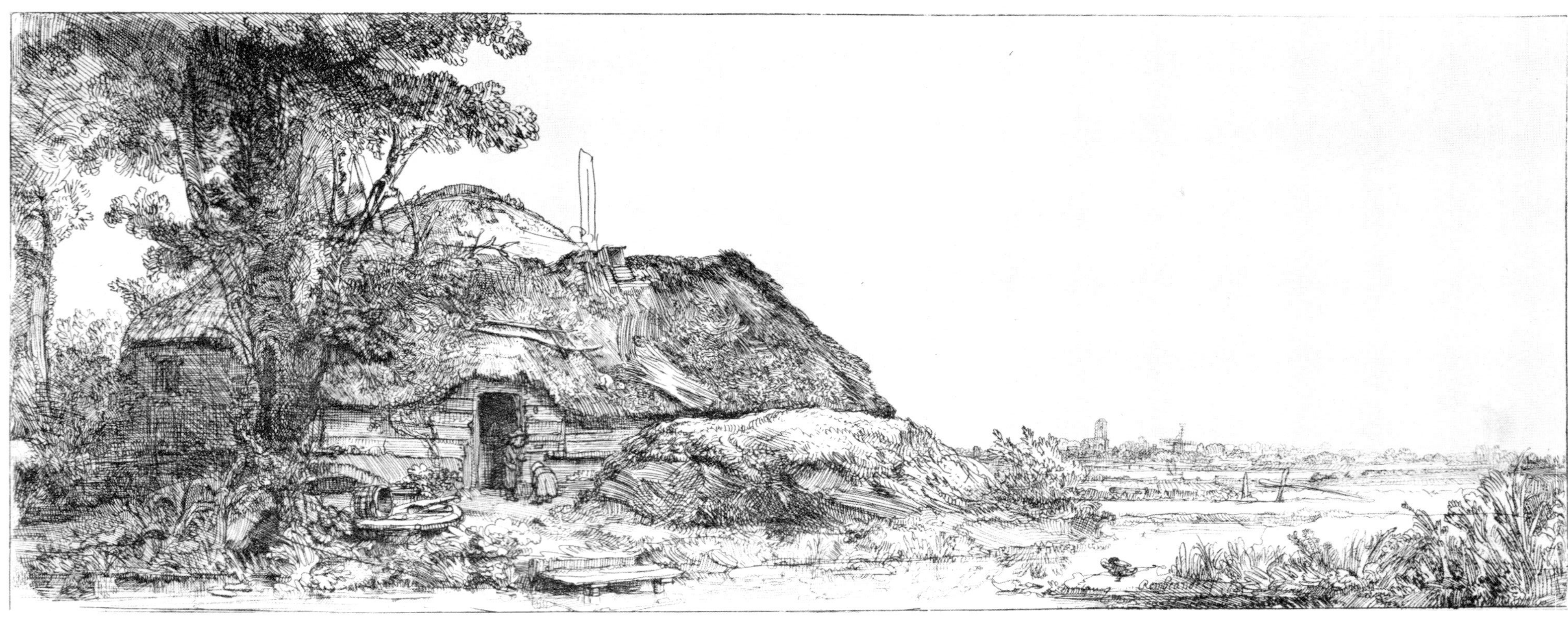

Landscape with cottage and haybarn. 1641.

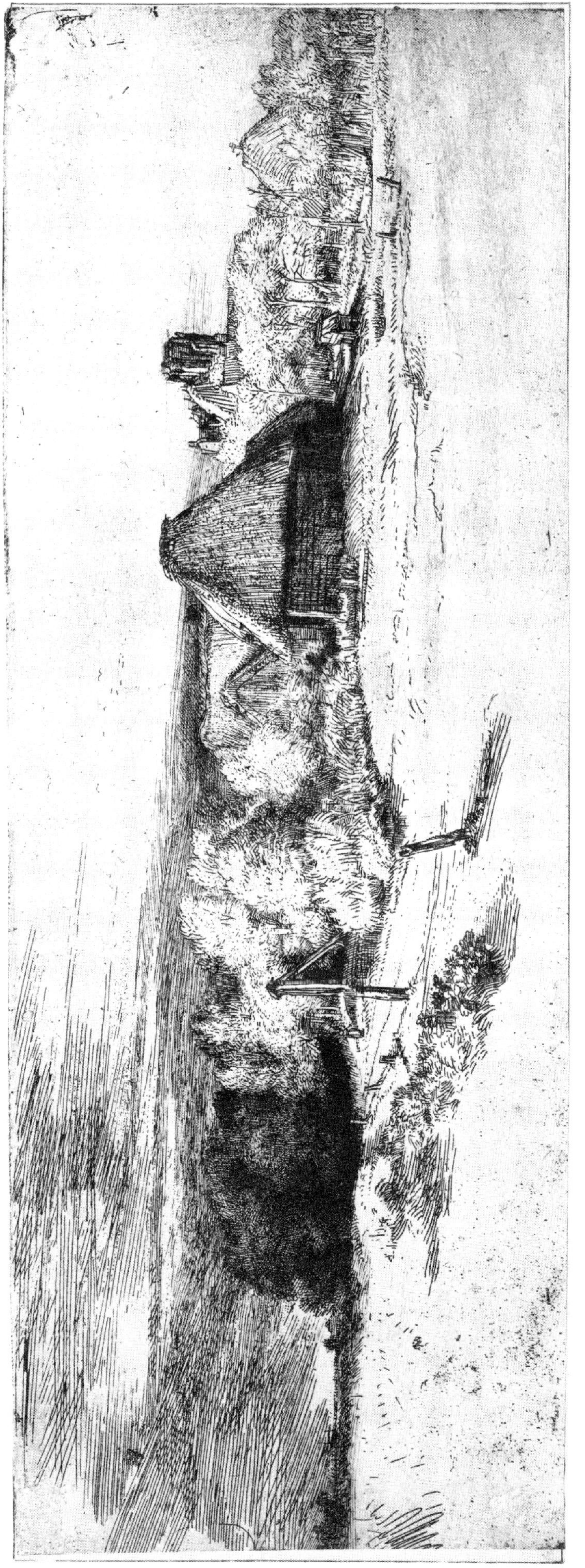

Landscape with trees, farm buildings and tower. 1650(?).

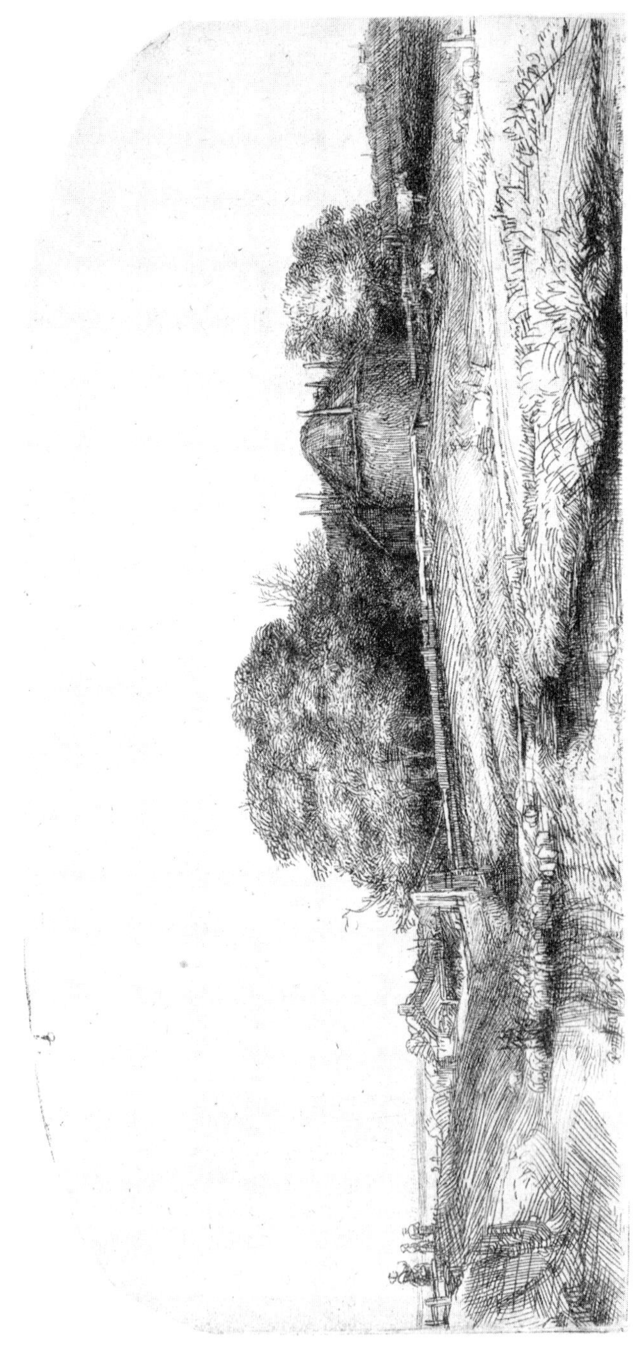

Landscape with haybarn and flock of sheep. 1652.

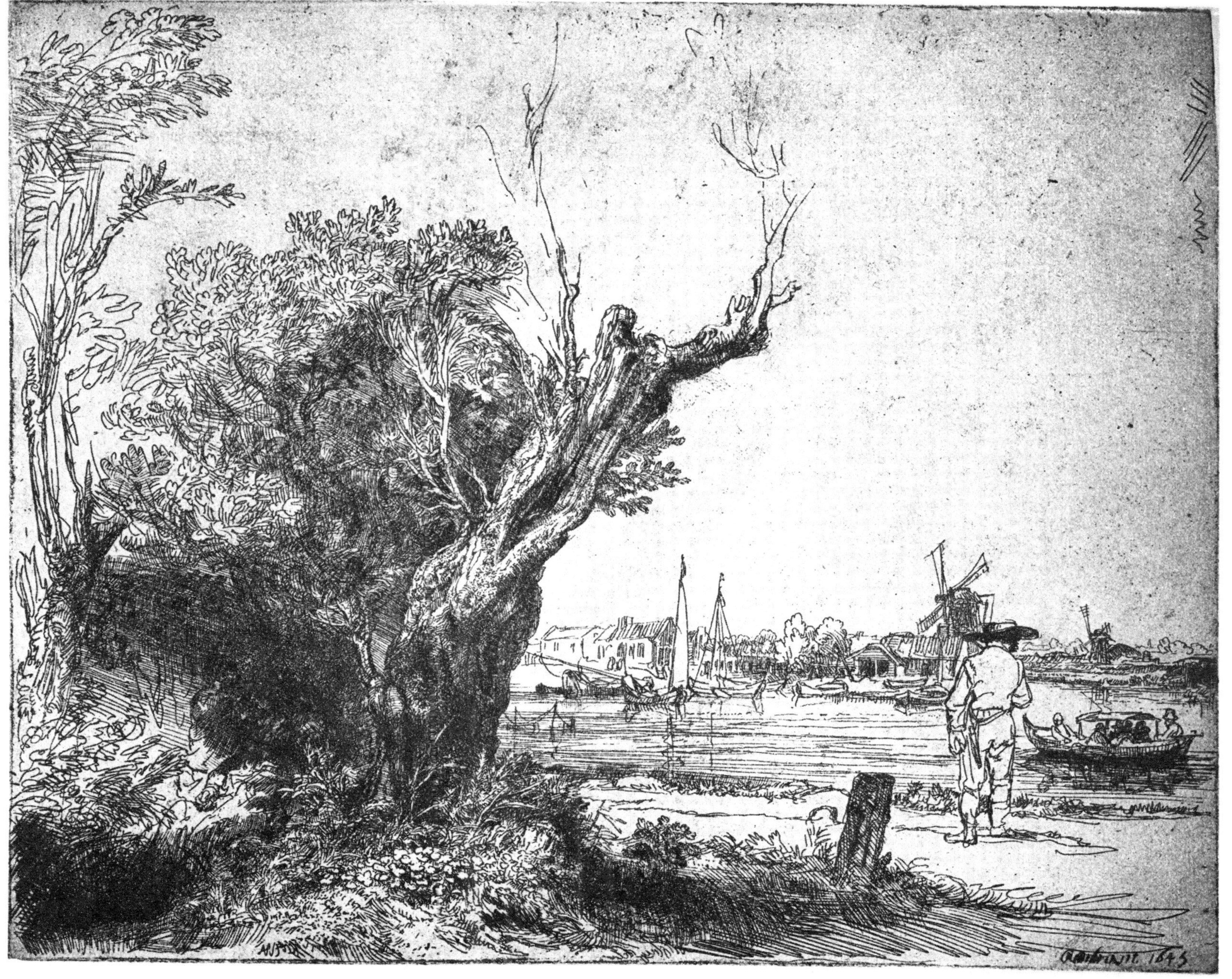

The Omval at the River Amstel. 1645.